Solomon and Pearl

May you always know the joy of being with Jesus. I wrote this for you.

The Practice of Being with Jesus

I have known Chris Cruz for 12 years and have had the great honor of watching him grow from a confident son to an empowering father — a leader who infuses and ignites that very confidence into a generation, that they may know their Creator as a Friend. In his first book, The Practice of Being with Jesus, Chris will guide you through simple-yet-transformative spiritual practices that will empower you to feel confident in your pursuit of the Lord. As Chris explains, if we're not intentionally choosing to be discipled by Jesus, then we are unintentionally being discipled by the world. I know that in the pages of this book you will find yourself resting daily in intimate connection with God's presence and trading busyness for true fulfillment. I highly recommend this book to the weary and hungry souls who are looking for practical and inspiring ways to pursue a joyful and wildly abundant life with Christ!

Kris Vallotton, Leader, Bethel Church, Redding, CA
Co-Founder of Bethel School of Supernatural Ministry
Author of thirteen books, including The Supernatural
Ways of Royalty, Heavy Rain and Poverty, Riches and
Wealth

I am so excited for this much needed book that Chris Cruz has written. It is so much more than another book to decorate your shelf; Chris has created a well worn path in these pages to discover the heart of God for yourself. This book is not more information to fill your head, but a tool that could bring radical transformation to your heart. If you dare to put into practice what's written in this book, you will never be the same.

Jonathan Helser, Co-Founder of the 18 Inch Journey and
Cageless Birds, Bethel Music Artist

I have had the ultimate privilege of watching Chris Cruz go from a young man to becoming one of the most dynamic leaders at Bethel. His passionate pursuit of God is evident in how he lives his life. This book is an expression of a deep seated value for following Jesus. The Practice of Being with Jesus is a message for a generation that longs to follow Jesus in the midst of endless options and a culture that is filled with unfulfilling static and noise. If you want to be a genuine follower of Jesus, this book is a brilliant place to start.

Eric Johnson, Senior Pastor Bethel Church

This is an extremely valuable equipping resource for anyone who longs for the more. One of our biggest challenges in modern culture is the act of being present. I believe Chris is addressing this and giving us tools for being with and following Jesus. The layout is simple, the truth is transforming, and the practices will lead you into a deeper walk with God.

Candace Johnson, Senior Pastor Bethel Church

There is a lot of theory about how to be with Jesus out there, as well as a massive hunger for His presence. But few folks have taken the time to make this practical and compelling. Chris has built something beautiful and simple to help us know and enjoy Jesus more.I believe this is going to help a lot of people move into true intimacy with Jesus.

Jon Tyson, Lead Pastor Church of the City New York

Chris has written a wise and practical book that will help you engage in vital daily spiritual practices.

Scott Harrison, New York Times Best-selling Author, THIRST- a Journey of Redemption, Compassion, and a Mission to Bring Clean Water to the World.

Pastor Chris is a leader and a true disciple of the faith who has cultivated in his own life the practice of spending time with Jesus. This book will position you to hear from God. In The Practice of Being with Jesus, Pastor Chris practically outlines what it looks like to practice being in His presence. Through intentional scripture reading, meditation, worship, silence, and prayer, you will experience the Holy Spirit discipling your heart, soul and mind.

Josh Kelsey, Senior Leader C3 NYC

In an age of digital distraction, hurriedness, and Biblical disinterest, The Practice of Being with Jesus offers a simple alternative for those longing to slow down and learn how to be with Jesus. This guide provides a helpful framework to encourage a daily life with Jesus through prayer, reading and meditating on Scripture, worship, and spiritual practices. I believe the Church needs this kind of transformative work to empower future generations to learn to live in loving union with God.

Darren Rouanzoin, Lead Pastor Garden Church

I have known Chris for over 10 years, and I have personally experienced the impact that his journey with The Lord has made on those around him, myself included. Because I know the fruit of Chris' life, I'm excited to endorse his new book, The Practice of Being with Jesus, which provides the reader with practical and profound insights into becoming a disciple of Christ. No matter where you are in your walk with Jesus, this book will help to develop and strengthen your relationship with Him. It is 28 days that will change your life!

Gabe Valenzula, Lead Overseer for Bethel School of Supernatural Ministry 2nd Year

Table of Contents

"I am with you always"
- Jesus

Foreword: Bill Johnson

The grace that introduced us to salvation is really only the beginning. God's intention for us is that by His grace we would be filled with His fullness. That is mind-boggling. He wants us to be filled not just with His Spirit but with His fullness!

We are empowered by His Spirit to do great things on the earth. But His love for us does not rise and fall, based on our performance. It is constant, as this is a relational journey that starts with His invitation of love.

We also know there is great reward for following Jesus. Yet if we follow Him for the sake of reward only, our foundation will be perilously fragile. That really is the point of Jesus' teaching, "Seek first the Kingdom . . . and all these things will be added." Without His priorities, we'll miss His intentions. We'll miss the point. We have been invited to follow Jesus simply for the joy of being with Him, while He in turn takes care of the other issues in life. That is the reason for the title, *The Practice of Being with Jesus*. It is the practice of His presence that awakens us to who we really are.

Chris Cruz has been a pastor in our environment for ten years. In that time, we have benefited greatly from his passion, focus, biblical teaching, and leadership skills. But I am most thankful for the way He values the presence of God above all else. In his wonderful book, *The Practice of Being with Jesus*, Chris gives the reader daily invitations into God's presence. Each of these movements provide rich insight into God's nature, His Covenant with us, and His intentions for the world.

As powerful as this book is, engaging with it entails no heavy requirements. In fact, all that is needed is a slight interest in spiritual growth. What is written will do the rest, as it is God who initiates this journey by inviting us into His presence just as we are. We are free to come to Him angry, bitter, brokenhearted, scared or immature. But He loves us too much to let us stay that way. We enter into the presence of the Lord and make an exchange. This is grace. Jesus says, "Come to Me, all you who labor and are heavy laden, and I will give you rest" (Matt. 11:28). We bring anxiety and fatigue, and He gives us His peace. In this journey, we receive constant upgrades for our lives that result in personal transformation.

And as we walk with Him, our prayer life also changes. We learn how to connect with His heart, releasing the Kingdom (His dominion) through our prayers. When we pray as servants, we find ourselves begging for the Master's intervention. But when we pray as sons and daughters, we join into a co-laboring role to see God's heart manifested on the earth in specific ways. Either will work. But He longs for us to come to Him as our Father. As we get to know His heart, we can persist in the pursuit of breakthrough in every situation until we see heaven invade our world. It's this revelation of His heart that endears us to the process. And that—shaping history through our intimate relationship with the Father—results in being filled with His fullness, the fullness of joy.

The Practice of Being with Jesus is a gift to the body Christ, inspiring and instructing us in our heart-to-heart connection to Jesus Christ. Complete abandonment to Him is the only logical result. Come to these pages with a heart open to the Holy Spirit. Ponder these truths, and absorb them deeply. It is from that place we are able to freely co-labor with God to release into the earth the transformation that we ourselves have experienced.

Bill Johnson
Bethel Church, Redding, CA
Author of *Hosting the Presence* and *The Way of Life*

"Come to Me."
- Jesus

Chapter One: My Story

You may not know much about me.

The odds are you barely know me at all. Yet, here we are with a book I wrote. So let's start with what might be an assumed statement, but a necessary one.

Jesus is everything to me.

This wasn't always true for me. I grew up going to church, but wasn't part of the church. I lived my own life with no real interest in Jesus. Then I had a life altering encounter. Now, when I think about Him my heart warms and worship flows from me.

It's hard to draw near to Him and not be undone. He has a way of making sense of my world by simply drawing near to me. In those moments I begin to realize that being with Him is enough. He calms me and leads me so well. He isn't afraid of my mess and doesn't abandon me in it. He speaks words I didn't know I needed to hear.

When I am in His presence my life begins to feel content. I am no longer scrambling, trying to cover up the aching of my soul for Him. I've come to realize that being in His presence is the reward of our relationship. He is such a kind and generous Father that He isn't content just giving me gifts. He wants to give me Himself. My other pursuits simply won't work well until I've cultivated being with Him.

I am different with Him. It's true.

I am tender because my guard is down. Jesus is safe; I've learned I don't have to wear armor. If I do come guarded, He disarms me in the right way. He shows me to myself so that I might be who He says I am. I sometimes cannot see the person I am meant to be until He shows me. I am shocked to realize I've been dreaming too small.

When I truly met Jesus I knew I couldn't live outside of Him. I was led to Him in a dramatic way–resulting in a hunger and thirst just to have a moment in His presence. I was bursting with a radical love for Him, and it kept increasing. I was drawn in more and more. My addictions and insecurities started to shed off me. Tasting the presence of Jesus is intoxicating. It was like breathing air for the first time. This happened for me in my living room.

I was gripped by Him. At first, I didn't want anything to do with Him, but He wanted everything to do with me. I grew up going to church, but I was lost, broken, and not committed. I became someone completely different that night.

My parents were hosting a small bible study in our home and friends of my aunt came to minister to people. Before that night, I'd never been prayed for or given a prophetic word. They asked me to come downstairs because I wasn't actually in the bible study. This was an unusual moment. I felt like I gave God an inch and He took a mile. I wasn't opposed to God, but I wasn't looking for Him. What was casual quickly became intense. They began to prophesy over me and something miraculous happened.

I felt this impending force. An immanent disruption. Then suddenly, He hit me and I lost control. I curled over in my chair. I was drowning in tears, and out of my mouth came a language I did not know I could speak. I was immersed in the Holy Spirit. I was burning with a sensation of fire, and a love so pure was radiating through my entire being.

God was cascading over me like a waterfall.

It was unlike anything I have ever experienced. It was raw, wild, and tender. I was shocked. I felt like a different person. As if I had never lived before. My insecurities faded into the background as I became aware of how much Jesus loved me. Consequently, I became enamoured with Jesus.

It was striking.

It wasn't progressive.

It was sudden.

My journey to wholeness took time, but my love for Him was ignited overnight. The presence of Jesus has a way of drawing out our radical love for Him. Here's the truth: Jesus is captivating, unless we're deceived. In that moment of my life the Holy Spirit revealed Jesus to me, and I've thirsted for Him ever since. I didn't thirst for an idea, a belief system, or a fancy sunday service. I couldn't even talk about Him without finding tears following hot on the heels of my words. I ached to be with Him. To know Him. To experience His love.

My encounter with the Holy Spirit started my journey of spending time alone with God.

I didn't have a church to go to– I only had my bedroom. I remember moments where God felt so close to me, I was terrified. The intimacy was so intense I would turn on all my lights. I actually cleared out my closet to become a meeting place for me and God. I grabbed a Bible, pillow and a headlamp. I was innocent, but I was ready to meet with God. I tasted His presence and there was no going back.

I just couldn't live without His presence.

We all intuitively know nothing compares to someone actually being with us. We know talking to a person is different than reading a letter from them. This is why videos of families being reunited with a parent who has been serving in the military make us cry. We all intuitively crave presence. Jesus draws us unto Him, and we cannot substitute being in His actual Presence. And in His presence, we're always transformed.

The hidden place of being with Jesus isn't the only place God changes us. But it's a crucial place for every believer–and God makes it available to everyone.

In spending time with Jesus, I began to learn from Him. Yet it wasn't always easy–as even the presence of God can become too familiar. I didn't start with much guidance, but I was hungry.

This unseen place of intimacy gains us no fame, but it transforms us. I wasn't doing it to hold up my external ministry. I did it to hold up my life. I became a witness to my own transformation by simply spending time with God.

Have you ever heard about the way bamboo trees grow? They can have no visible height increase for up to 5 years as they grow their roots.

If you were to measure the success of a bamboo tree against the height of other plants or trees, you might consider the bamboo a failure. But underneath the surface, it is creating what will sustain its inevitable growth. Then, in a matter of weeks, the bamboo will skyrocket up to 80 feet. The long process of hidden growth sustains its visible life. The same is true for our spirituality.

I worked in a school of ministry for seven years with students from around the world. One of the most common questions was, "What does your alone time with God look like?" They knew they needed time with God, but were unsure of how to do it. They felt like the disciples asking Jesus to teach them how to pray. And if we recall the story, Jesus didn't tell them to simply talk to God. He gave them a path of sorts. He gave them what we call the Lord's Prayer. It's not the only way to pray, but it was a framework for prayer. I'd call it a liturgy that shaped the disciples as they prayed it.

This book follows in that concept of giving disciples a path for prayer. The Practice of Being with Jesus is made up of movements that are formative steps to help give intentionality to your time with Him. The movements in this book are not the only way to spend time with God–but they have been tested, and they work.

The movements in this daily practice are thoughtful and formative. They create space for Jesus in our life. They aren't magic. They require your heart to be present and open. If you engage in a framework motivated by ritual instead love, then you will find these practices unfruitful.

I wrote this little book because I think being with Jesus is the greatest joy of a disciple's life. A disciple of Jesus prioritizes being with Him. There's nothing like His presence in this life. I want you to enjoy Him and have confidence in spending time with Him.

Let's be disciples who draw near to Him before we do anything else.

Chapter Two: Life As A Disciple

You are becoming someone.

Every second of every hour; every hour of every day; every day of every week; every week of every month; every month of every year; and every year of your life you're becoming someone.

The great risk is not thinking twice about who you're becoming because you're too consumed with what you're doing in life. You can become so swarmed by the demands of everyday life that you pay no attention to your spiritual life.

Our modern culture has an insatiable appetite and will devour whatever time we haven't intentionally alloted to meaningful pursuits. The unfulfilled life has its own gravitational pull–its own negative energy. Unless we act intentionally, we will be consumed by the trivial and neglect the eternal. The only remedy is to replace that life.

But what kind of life will be enough for us?

Jesus said, *"It is enough for a disciple to be like his teacher."*

A life becoming like Jesus is the satisfaction we're longing for today. Jesus is the epitome of human life. Salvation isn't simply the forgiveness of sin but the receiving of Jesus' very own life as our own.

I think discipleship, as made known by Jesus, is the cure for the human condition.

It's the cure for the rushed life.

It's the cure for the anxious life.

It's the cure for the fearful life.

It's the cure for the angry life.

It's the cure for the shameful life.

It's the cure for the human life.

If discipleship to Jesus really is the cure then we need to re-discover what it means to be a disciple.

What does it mean to be a disciple of Jesus?

Most people have a narrow view of discipleship. It's often thought of as a six-week program for new believers, or what you do when you get serious about Jesus, or a method for church growth. All of those things are good– but they aren't what Jesus had in mind.

First off, Jesus didn't invent the word "disciple".

We've become overly familiar with the word, and it has lost its potency. Disciples existed before Jesus was ever born. John the Baptist, Jewish Rabbis, and Greek philosophers all had disciples.

A disciple, simply put, is a learner of an embodied way of life. A disciple is someone who subjects themselves to the way of their master. This master defines their ideal life, and how to live in it. A disciple trusts a master's definition of reality, and organizes their life around becoming like their master and learning from them.

Discipleship is about discovering what kind of life you're going to live. Jesus comes as the Master of life itself, embodying God's reality. Jesus claims this life is available in the here and now. Jesus didn't just come announcing forgiveness. He came announcing the availability of living in the Kingdom of God.

As disciples of Jesus, we become His students. We learn how to live in the Kingdom of God. The Kingdom of God is the home for our soul. We're designed to flourish in it like plants in good soil. We thrive if we have proper relationship to the Kingdom of God. If we do not learn how to live in the Kingdom, we'll be stunted, never quite becoming who we're meant to be in this life.

As a disciple of Jesus, you're set free from the kingdom of darkness and of your old self. You're brought into the Kingdom of God and your new self. Jesus announces God is rescuing you from the human you were never meant to be, in order to become the human He first dreamed you to be.

This is salvation.

It includes all the things you were taught about eternal security and forgiveness, but it is also so much more.

Salvation isn't about managing a broken life and simply claiming that you're forgiven. Salvation is replacing your old life with a new one. Trusting in Jesus makes the cosmic healing, made available to us on the cross, known in us personally.

When we trust in Jesus, we receive His life and become devoted recipients of His way of being in the world. He carved out a human path for fulfillment in God. He invites us to follow Him into His good life—here and now.

What does this good life look like?

It looks like progressively and holistically having the mind, character, emotions, habits, relationships, ministry, and leadership of Jesus embodied in our lives. It looks like living in unceasing union with the Father. We continually live out of our new self, made in the image of Jesus. We stop living under the influence of lies about God, ourselves, and the world.

This good life is the way of true wholeness.

Your entire being starts to transform. You start becoming a new human. You carry the peace Jesus carried. You become generous like Him. You respond to situations as He responded to situations. You care for people as He did. And this doesn't happen by willpower. It happens by surrender.

But this good life doesn't grow in us by accident.

Jesus calls us to be intentional students of His life. We become learners of His way. We become people who practice Jesus' teaching and follow His example. We become disciples of Jesus. We don't just imitate His actions–we seek to understand His ways. Discipleship creates the space for grace to transform us to the point where we naturally do what Jesus did.

This invitation to be discipled by Jesus is nothing short of having a different quality of life. The disciple of Jesus orders their life differently. If we desire to have the spiritual life of Jesus, we must begin to implement the overall lifestyle of Jesus.

Christ is being formed within us. We see the evidence of this in our increasing love for God and others. Spiritual exercises, modeled after the lifestyle of Jesus, create a type of receptacle for the Holy Spirit to give us the abundant life of Jesus. We cannot become a disciple by accident. If we're not intentionally being discipled by Jesus then we are unintentionally being discipled by the world.

Therefore, be with Jesus

Chapter Three: The Practice

We cannot be a disciple of Jesus from a distance. If our aim is to be possessed by Jesus it must be through intimate knowledge. As A. W. Tozer once said, *"God is a person and, as such, can be cultivated as any person can. It is inherent in personality to be able to know another personality, but full knowledge of one's personality by another cannot be achieved by one encounter."* This is a friendship. A consistent interactive union with Him. An intimate knowledge of God may start by having a radical encounter with God, but it is sustained through daily devotion unto God.

The quality of life we all dream of as disciples is tethered to being with Jesus. Our journey of holistic change begins with Jesus inviting us to first be with Him. I say "intentionally" because this will not happen by accident or chance. How can I long to know Jesus while never setting aside time to be with Him? My longing, then, would actually be a way to make me feel like a better Christian instead of an actual longing for Him. I might not start with longing. I might start with curiosity, perhaps. But my desire for God will grow into a longing through cultivation.

The source of our longing is God's desire to manifest Himself to us. It precedes and initiates our own desire for Him. We are never outside of experiencing God's presence, but our experience of His presence differs. As my pastor, Bill Johnson, says, *"God has been given to us without measure, but we set the limits of that measure. Though all of the measurements are set up on our end of the equation, we can experience the measure of presence we are willing to jealously guard. Whatever you will jealousy guard, that is the measure you will have on a consistent basis."* The practice of being with Jesus is a way to jealously guard the presence of God in your life.

I use the word "practice" purposefully. A practice is a deliberate act of engagement with an activity, for the purpose of enjoying, strengthening, and mastering that activity. When I am "practicing" being with Jesus, I am wanting to enjoy His presence. I am strengthening my relationship with Him, and mastering the art of submitting myself to His presence. I once heard that "Practice doesn't make perfect–it makes possible". In this case, the practice of spending time with Jesus makes the vibrant life we're looking for possible.

A life with Jesus isn't theoretical or abstract. You should be able to know whether or not you are or aren't spending time with Him. This doesn't mean you embrace the monastic life and spend twenty-four hours alone–but it also doesn't mean you only interact with God's presence during your Sunday morning church attendance.

The New Testament writers use training language to ensure that our faith is not merely a set of beliefs–it must also be expressed through our practices. Orthodoxy matters, but so does orthopraxy. Orthopraxy is a way for us to embody what we believe. It is expressing our beliefs in an intentional way throughout our everyday life as a disciple.

The Apostle Paul tells Timothy, *"Train yourself in godliness."*

In Paul's letter to the Corinthians, he tells them they're running a race–and they should race to win by being a person who is *"disciplined in their training."*

Paul instructs the Philippains to take *"Whatever you have learned or received or heard from me, or seen in me, put [it] into practice." Jesus said, "Everyone then who hears these words of mine and puts them into practice is like a wise man who built his house on the rock."*

Practice isn't about perfection but progress. This book is built around the practice of being with Jesus, which has been the anchor of my spiritual life. It's not the only thing I do with God, but it's one of the most important things I do with Him.

Spending time with God is also one of the easiest things to let go of. It becomes a place of discouragement to us, as we live rushed lives that demand more and more from us. I want to help you close the gap between intending to spend time with God, and actually implementing the practice of His presence.

A.W Tozer is one of my heroes of the spiritual life. I've been lead into some of the deepest encounters with God through his books. He never pulled punches, and what he wrote still pierces my soul. He said, *"It is well that we accept the hard truth now: the man who would know God must give time to Him! He must count no time wasted which is spent in the cultivation of His acquaintance. He must give himself to medi-*

tation and prayer hours on end. So did the saints of old, the glorious company of the apostles, the godly fellowship of the prophets and the believing members of the holy Church in all generations. And so must we if we would follow in their train! May not the inadequacy of much of our spiritual experience be traced back to our habit of skipping through the corridors of the Kingdom like little children through the marketplace, chattering about everything but pausing to learn the true value of nothing?"

Intimacy with God has no shortcuts. The practice of being with Jesus has a concrete application. Our relationship with Him flourishes as we give real space to be with Him. Our intention to be in His presence won't quench our soul's thirst. The sporadic moments are treasures, but I can't build my intimacy with Him on those. I need to give actual set aside time to knowing Him where He is my focus.

This might sound harsh. I don't intend it to be. But Jesus doesn't get the crumbs from our table. We organize our lives around what sustains and deepens intimacy with Him. We need to get to a place where we can honestly say, "My life is nothing without Him." Can we dare to believe one day with Him is better than a thousand elsewhere?

We must cultivate our longing to be in His presence. We need to have Him wash over us with His love and cast out all our fears. He is our hiding place. He needs to be the one we run to. Everything is different when we're with Him.

The good news is that Jesus waits patiently for us. He is not offended by our skipping along through life. He stands at the door and knocks. He isn't going anywhere. He has made up His mind. He wants to be with us.

The practice of spending time with Jesus has been emphasized by many, but not often explained. We're told we need to spend time with God—and that's about it. It's like telling a starving infant they need to eat something. Though the diagnosis might be right, the instruction is unhelpful without guidance. It can feel obvious, yet remain elusive and unattainable without guidance.

When time with Jesus remains mysterious and not practical, it can cause people to make a lot of unnecessary assumptions. They think, "I just need to pray more." Then most people end up praying for fifteen minutes to recycle through their prayer list , and they leave feeling bored. They don't know how to be alone with Jesus.

The secret place of God's presence isn't the same as a large gathering. We don't have a loud worship team and hundreds of other voices. It's just us and God. It's raw and unnerving at times. We have to press through what initially might feel dull. We can become accustomed to God's presence feeling a certain way with other people around us. The daily practice might feel monotonous. A rhythmic spiritual life can quickly feel like we're going through the motions. I promise it will become lively if you remain with Him. Can you resist the need for God to come in a chariot of fire, whirlwind, or earthquake? If God wants to reveal Himself as a real person in our midst, we must be willing to know Him in whatever way He reveals Himself.

Many disciples have abandoned the essential practice of being in God's presence because they are defeated by their own boredom. Others have tried to avoid this discouragement by changing the format of their time with God. After all," they think, "Doesn't God go with me everywhere? Why not just do what I enjoy while I know He's with me? Perhaps I could go kayaking instead of sitting here reading in silence.

Kayaking with God is a grand idea–and I am sure it's very fun–but it cannot replace an actual concrete moment devoted to be with, learn from, and express love to Jesus. Quality time sometimes requires my full attention and devotion. This practice isn't impossible, but it can initially feel taxing. It always takes a measure of effort whenever we start a new habit. Such an effort creates space for the thing we value. I love what Dallas Willard said about grace. He said, *"Grace isn't opposed to effort, it's opposed to earning."* That is profound! When we embrace the training perspective of the New Testament, we embrace a new commitment to retrain our habits. Jesus is calling you to Him. He is patient, but accepts no substitute for quality time with you.

He does not want to be a bystander in your life. He wants to give you Himself, and He wants you in the exchange.

There's no doubt that a person daring to be with Jesus will experience a new kind of existence. A life embodying peace, rest, contentment, passion, joy–and fun. A life where you are naturally living as Jesus lived, and doing the things He did.

You can do the things Jesus did without spending any time with Jesus. But it will eventually betray you. If you do the things Jesus did without being with Him, you will make more withdrawals than deposits and eventually go bankrupt. You will have a shell of Jesus's life, but not the essence of it. You will be productive but you won't be fulfilled.

The only way to be fulfilled in this life is to practice being with Jesus. He says, "Come to me," not "Do more work." He is the fountain of water that keeps us living. This is not a requirement—it's a privilege.

We must first get out of doing more for Jesus, and make sure we're thriving with Jesus. This book is a companion guide into the mystery of being with Him. I am trying to help both ends of the spectrum: the discouraged disciple who has never found a rhythm, and the seasoned follower looking for refreshment.

A few points for the road ahead. You'll need to determine where you're going to spend time with Jesus while going through this book. This book will help you quickly engage with God, so it helps to already have a place and time set aside for yourself. A fixed time and place makes it easier for you to practice these disciplines, so you don't have to make the same decision again and again. My final suggestion is to decide on how long you spend time with Jesus each time. I suggest no less than 15 minutes for this practice. You don't need to spend an hour, but it needs to be long enough to allow for real relationship to flourish. If Jesus is knocking on your door, welcome Him in for at least as long as you would a friend stopping by your home address.

What lies ahead of you is worth the sacrifice of your time. You will be changed by the knowledge of God, and you will grow by what God reveals to you about yourself. But most importantly, so will your love for Jesus.

Chapter Four: Posture of Heart

As we get closer to starting the practice, we need to cover some inner postures that will guide you through the days ahead.

God wants to be with You

The practice of being with Jesus must stand on something solid. Our perspective of God is the foundation of our time with Him. I will hit this multiple times in the devotionals ahead, but let me say this upfront: God desires to be with you.

You're not intolerable to Him. He doesn't endure you–He enjoys you. Jesus isn't the kind of friend who counts the minutes until He can leave your presence. Intimacy is His idea. We honestly only crave intimacy with Jesus to the degree we're awakened to His desire to be with us. He is persistent and available, not reluctant and withdrawn.

God is giddy for you to be with Him. He wants to speak to you. We don't need to convince Him. We enter into His presence already loved by Him. As Martin Luther said, *"Prayer is not overcoming the reluctance of God. It's laying hold to His willingness."* We open ourselves up to His desire for us.

Remember the Goal

The goal isn't to get through the movements, but rather be with Jesus. If you begin the practice and you get an unusual or overwhelming sense of Jesus' presence, then please close the book and be with Him. If He is washing over you with His love, then don't change the pace. This won't happen every time–but it's important to surrender when it does happen. You shouldn't be looking to just complete the movements without actually engaging with Jesus. It's possible to breeze through them and have a sense of satisfaction that comes from completing a task. This isn't a task. We're not looking to make this a chore. I want this book to be a path into God's presence, and a tool for spiritual formation. Please slow down if you find the temptation to rush through the exercises. His presence in the goal.

Follow the Spirit

If you start this journey, and the Spirit is redirecting you while in the practice, then listen to Him. If He is leading you to do something else, follow Him. I always want your time to be submitted to His voice over a structure. We want to be awake to His Spirit and recognize He is leading us. We come with our intentionality, but He brings His direction. But be mindful: if this happens every time, then you might need to ask yourself if you're afraid to trust He will meet you through the structure instead of just the spontaneity.

Remain Prayerful

As you start, remain prayerful. This means always ready to engage with prayer. If the Spirit draws you into intercession then focus on intercession. God might interrupt your flow to draw you into a moment of prayer. It's important to follow these leadings. God might highlight something to draw you in deeper. Go ahead and partner with Him by praying into what He is showing you or bringing to your attention. This can be a simple moment–but it can also be a larger course-changing burden of prayer. Be ready to pause the practice to engage with what Jesus is revealing to you.

Honest

You must commit to honesty even if it hurts you. Jesus doesn't heal our egos. He doesn't polish our masks. This means you'll have to forgo pleasure and "happiness" so that you can be free. Humans have been crippled by the temptation to hide themselves since the garden. Honesty requires courage. It's one of the bravest choices we can make in life. Jesus isn't afraid of the "real" us–but He can only heal what we are willing to reveal.

Recognize Your Desires

What is it that you want? What's the core desire of your life? Jesus wants to engage with that desire. Our deepest desires go beyond our materialistic possessions. Jesus often asked the unmistakably sick what they wanted from Him. Even though their pain was apparent, Jesus invited them to grow by vocalizing their deepest desire. If we name our desires, we increase our intimacy with God. If we hide them, our relationship remains distant. We cannot assume "God already knows", even though He does. Our intimacy grows as our vulnerability increases. If we only share what our ego desires, we will feel more spiritual but we may never get free.

Patience

We have to let go of performance-based religion. We're not doing this to earn love, but to progressively open ourselves up to the love we've already been given. You might miss days, or struggle with practicing silence. We're not in this for perfection but progress. I love what Richard Foster says: "We're training harder, not trying harder." This is about retraining ourselves–and that takes time. Please don't let discouragement win. It's normal to set goals and have set-backs. We just have to remain patient. I define patience as unwavering loyalty. We're in this for a life with Jesus.

All Day

We spend time with Jesus to reorient ourselves in order to live our life well. This isn't about charging your battery at the beginning of the day and draining it throughout the day. We don't start to then become drained. The goal is to remain full. A great woman of Church history named Jean Guyon describes it like this: *"It's not enough to be turned inwardly to your Lord an hour or two each day. There is little value in being turned within to the Lord unless the end result is an anointing and a spirit of prayer which continues with you during the whole day."*

Chapter Five: The Daily Movements

Presence

We begin by becoming aware of being with Jesus. We need to start consciously engaging with Him as a person who is present with us. We open ourselves to Him and start our time centering ourselves in the reality of being in His Presence. We begin to contemplate His nearness. This is engaging our heart and our mind with Jesus, and it moves us toward experiencing Him. This can be a few minutes or quite a bit more–but we begin and end the practice here.

Silence

We all have a desire to free ourselves from the distractions and the busyness that keeps us from being present. Silence is when we intentionally position ourselves to be present to God beyond our words. Jean Guyon describes the importance of silence like this: *"When He desires to speak to you, He demands the most intense attention to his voice."* We don't rush and overwork our mind to feel peace. We rest in His Presence like a child who is totally safe. Incidentally, we also become more aware of ourselves in silence–but growing more attentive to God's voice, and surrendering more of ourselves to His will, is the greatest fruit of this practice. It's a deep and powerful abiding. This part might be the hardest movement at first because we're so unfamiliar with being silent. It will take time but eventually, it will be so refreshing.

Worship

We're a habitation for His Presence. This cannot take place to the measure God has in mind without the priority of worship. Worship is not only thanking Him for what He has done–it's passionately expressing our desire for Him and His utmost place in our lives. Worship is our response to His worth. Worship is how we treasure His Presence with us. We become awed by His nearness and fall deeper in love with Him.

Psalm

The Psalms was the worship and prayer book for Jesus and early Christians. They still teach us how to pray. As Dallas Willard said, *"If you bury yourself in Psalms, you emerge knowing God and understanding life. We learn from the Psalms how to think and act in reference to God. We drink in God and God's world from them. They provide a vocabulary for living Godward."* In this book, we will go through four Psalms in total–focusing on a new Psalm at the beginning of each week. This movement should help us keep a worshipful posture as we go through the other movements.

Gospel

The four Gospels tell the good news of Jesus. We learn that God has irreversibly done reconciling work in the world through Jesus. They share with us Jesus's life, teachings, death, and resurrection from four unique vantage points. The Gospels lead us to trust in Him as Lord. When we read the Gospels we learn from Jesus, become like Jesus, and get empowered to live as Jesus lived. In this daily practice, we will read through the Gospel according to Matthew.

Meditation

The purpose of meditation is to enable us to hear God clearly. Meditation is listening, sensing, and pondering Christ. This isn't studying. This isn't an intellectual exercise. This is a contemplative and imaginative practice. We open ourselves up to be apprehended by Him through recalling and reflecting upon Jesus. Thomas A Kempis calls meditation *"a familiar friendship with Jesus."* Meditation is a spiritual practice that helps us to eliminate hurry, slow down, pause, listen well, and hear correctly in order to awaken to the presence of God and receive His rest. We will have a verse each day for us to meditate on. You do not need to study this verse or take notes on it. Simply be present to God as you savor it.

Scripture

Scripture serves many purposes. One of those purposes is to provide a framework for edification and growth. The daily scripture is the root of the devotional writing that follows. Scripture helps us grasp and apply the truth the Holy Spirit leads us into.

Devotional

As disciples who spend time with Jesus, we learn. These following devotionals are daily movements that unpack the daily reading of Scripture. This is for spiritual edification rather than doctrinal instruction. They aren't meant to begin an in-depth study. Rather, the devotional is meant to accompany what we learn from Jesus while we are with Him.

Questions

We would often see Jesus ask disciples questions. The questions He asked would cause His listeners to reflect, to be honest, look within, and be reformed. Jesus would upset people with questions because their answers revealed their hearts. Jesus wanted to get at the root of the spiritual condition of His hearers, and He often would use questions to arrive there. We ask ourselves daily questions to bring us to the heart of the matter, and to create deeper vulnerability before the Lord

Prayer

When Jesus' disciples asked Him to teach them how to pray, He gave them an actual prayer. Jesus didn't say, "Prayer is just talking to God." Jesus gave them a liturgy to pray. It was something that guided them because He wanted them to be shaped by the words He crafted. Though God always welcomes the spontaneity of our heart's confession, it is deeply formative to submit ourselves to a written liturgy of prayer. The included daily prayer helps us engage with what we learn in the devotional.

Week One

Presence

Jesus, be with me. My life is nothing without You. I long to be in Your Presence, where I find true rest. Wash over me with Your love, and cast out all of my fears. You're my safety. You're my hiding place. You're the one I run to. Everything is different when I am with You. As I rest here with You, overshadow me with Your loving Presence.

Silence

2 minutes of sitting in silence being present to Jesus and yourself.

Worship

Tell Jesus the place He has in your life and what He means to you.

Meditation

Matthew 11:28-30

Read it. Pray it. Ponder it.

"Come to me, all you who are weary and burdened, and I will give you rest. Take my yoke upon you and learn from me, for I am gentle and humble in heart, and you will find rest for your souls. For my yoke is easy and my burden is light."

Scripture: 1 Kings 19:11-13

[11] He said, "Go out and stand on the mountain before the Lord, for the Lord is about to pass by." Now there was a great

wind, so strong that it was splitting mountains and breaking rocks in pieces before the Lord, but the Lord was not in the wind; and after the wind an earthquake, but the Lord was not in the earthquake; [12] and after the earthquake a fire, but the Lord was not in the fire; and after the fire a sound of sheer silence. [13] When Elijah heard it, he wrapped his face in his mantle and went out and stood at the entrance of the cave. Then there came a voice to him that said, "What are you doing here, Elijah?" (NIV)

Devotional: Silence and Solitude

God can be known.

We are transformed by being in His presence. A trusted path into the knowledge of God is to withdraw into silence and solitude. We create space for Him by stepping away from the day-to-day human interactions that can actually lock us into unhealthy ways of living. We withdraw from the world to draw close to Him. We undo any hold the world has on us to be held by Him.

We can avoid the secret place of solitude and silence with God. We fear the pruning of our desire for fame, praise, and significance. Jesus would often withdraw from the crowds who placed strong demands upon Him. Jesus withdrew to give God times of undivided attention. Without them, He was vulnerable to the pressures and expectations of others.

We can be tempted to build our life on "open rewards"–but that's not how God wants to build it. He wants the secret place to be our reward. It's in the willingness to be silent before Him that we begin to recognize the chatter that plagues us, and the significance we gain from what we hear from others.

Ruth Hayley Barton said, *"The practices of solitude and silence are radical because they challenge us on every level of our existence. They challenge us on the level of culture: there is little in Western culture that supports us in entering into what feels like unproductive time for being (beyond human effort) and listening (beyond human thought). They confront us on the level of our human relationships: they call us away from those relationships for a time so we can give undivided attention to God. They challenge us on the level of our soul: in the silence we become aware of inner dynamics we have been able to avoid by keeping ourselves noisy and busy. They draw us into spiritual battle: in silence there is the potential for each of us to 'know that I am God' with such certainty that the competing powers of evil and sin and the ego-self can no longer hold us in their grip. All forces of evil band together to prevent our knowing God in this way, because it brings to an end the dominion of those powers in our lives."*

The power of solitude and silence is also in stopping whatever we're using to distract us from ourselves. We stop turning to excitement and mindless activities to recalibrate our soul. Sometimes we think that all we need is more downtime in our day in order to feel rested. But this a myth: we would just fill our schedule. We have to release some things in order to have rest.

When we go to solitude and silence, we find God—and, in turn, we find ourselves. He rescues us from our distracted existence. We withdraw with Him and, in being still before Him, we stop letting our culture's obsession with accomplishments and busyness have its way with us.

God is a friend who knows everything going on in our lives—

and He allows us to just sit there and not explain. He eventually speaks into those moments because we have stopped talking long enough to be receptive. We begin to become the ones who listen to God, instead of those who talk at God.

The beginning of sitting in silence with God is hard. We're trained to use our words with Him. We don't know what to do with pure Presence. We can't sit with ourselves, let alone God. When we are finally silent, God asks us questions. Similar to Elijah, the distractions end and God is found in the sheer silence. With Elijah, God's first question is profound. He asks, "What are you doing here?"

God wants an honest answer as to why we're coming to Him. Solitude and silence allow the space for us to finally be honest with God, because the distractions are gone–and we're safe with Him.

Question

Why are you alone in God's presence today?

Prayer

God, I sit with You. I listen for Your voice. I respond honestly, withholding nothing from You. God, I desire to know You fully. God, I am desperate for Your pure Presence. It is there that You set me free. I am free from distractions. I am free from bondage. I am alive to Your safety. I am sharing in Your truth. God, I am made to be in union with You and I will never rush from Your presence. Amen.

Silence

2 minutes of sitting in silence being present to Jesus and yourself.

Presence

Holy Spirit lead me.
Holy Spirit sustain me.
Holy Spirit move through me.

Presence

Jesus, be with me. My life is nothing without You. I long to be in Your Presence, where I find true rest. Wash over me with Your love, and cast out all of my fears. You're my safety. You're my hiding place. You're the one I run to. Everything is different when I am with You. As I rest here with You, overshadow me with Your loving Presence.

Silence

2 minutes of sitting in silence being present to Jesus and yourself.

Worship

Tell Jesus the place He has in your life and what He means to you.

Meditation

Matthew 11:28-30

Read it. Pray it. Ponder it.

Psalm of the week **23**

Matthew 2

"Come to me, all you who are weary and burdened, and I will give you rest. Take my yoke upon you and learn from me, for I am gentle and humble in heart, and you will find rest for your souls. For my yoke is easy and my burden is light."

Scripture: Matthew 6:25-26

[25] Therefore I tell you, do not worry about your life, what you will eat or drink; or about your body, what you will wear. Is not life more important than food, and the body more important than clothes? [26] Look at the birds of the air; they do not sow or reap or store away in barns, and yet your heavenly Father feeds them. Are you not much more valuable than they?" (NIV)

Devotional: Simplicity

The world can define a good life by how many things you own, how many things you have going for you, or how productive you are in a day. But these definitions make for a cluttered life.

Our rushed lives move without any awareness of our soul. We're bound by our possessions and pursuits. Our minds feel cluttered, and we're confused as to why we feel absent to the things that matter. We avoid the feeling of emptiness inside of us with our lust for more. We're scared to face the emptiness we might feel, so we overindulge. We're in bondage, but think we're living the good life.

Jesus defines the good life as being free.

The freedom Jesus offers is the opportunity to live in the unceasing love of God. It is being convinced He is for you. It's trusting Him so that your soul can be content–enjoying and sharing all you have in this life.

You are not entangled by the drive to make your life a spectacle.

You are not entangled by an insatiable need for things.

You are not entangled by fear of not having or being enough.

You are not entangled by doing more to feel more important.

We can journey into this kind of life by the intentional practice of simplicity.

The spiritual practice of simplicity is an attitude of gratitude that flows into generosity. It's letting go, and loosening our grip on, any attachments we might have to owning or hoarding our blessings.

Richard Foster said, *"Simplicity sets possessions in proper perspective. Simplicity is the only thing that sufficiently reorients our lives so that possessions can be genuinely enjoyed without destroying us."*

Simplicity flows from focusing on what matters most, so lesser matters lose their grip on us. We're not owned by the good things we have in life. We live content in what God has provided. We live resting in our identity. We share what we have been given, because our blessings flow through us.

This is what it means to seek first the Kingdom of God.

If you seek first the Kingdom then everything else will be added to you.

If you seek everything else then the Kingdom of God may never be found in you.

We need to examine our lives. We need to scrutinize our attachments. Anthony de Mello said, *"If you look carefully you will see that there is one thing that causes unhappiness. The name of that thing is Attachment. What is an attachment? An emotional state of clinging caused by the belief that without some particular thing or some person you cannot be happy."*

Simplicity is about trusting God to be enough—and if that means we have to let go of some stuff, then so be it. The goal isn't just to let go. It's to be inwardly focused on God and on His sufficiency for us.

You will find sustained joy and contentment by intentionally letting go of secondary things, so that the primary things can have their proper place.

Question

Which attachments in your life does the Lord want you to let go of?

___

Prayer
God, I feel You in the stillness and settle my heart and soul. Clear my vision and make known to me any unhealthy attachments—for Your redemptive plan has always made me whole. I am trusting that You are enough, and nothing else will ever satisfy. God, You are at the center of my life, and it is from You that all blessings flow. I cast my cares, I release my dreams, and I abandon my desires to be found in You. God, teach me what it means to be fully focused. Teach me what it means to be fully known. I am thankful that I hear Your voice. God, I am here to experience Your presence and to let go of control. Amen.

Silence
2 minutes of sitting in silence being present to Jesus and yourself.

Presence

Holy Spirit lead me.
Holy Spirit sustain me.
Holy Spirit move through me.

Week One

Day 03

Presence

Jesus, be with me. My life is nothing without You. I long to be in Your Presence, where I find true rest. Wash over me with Your love, and cast out all of my fears. You're my safety. You're my hiding place. You're the one I run to. Everything is different when I am with You. As I rest here with You, overshadow me with Your loving Presence.

Silence

2 minutes of sitting in silence being present to Jesus and yourself.

Worship

Tell Jesus the place He has in your life and what He means to you.

Psalm of the week **23**

Matthew 3

Meditation

Matthew 11:28-30

Read it. Pray it. Ponder it.

"Come to me, all you who are weary and burdened, and I will give you rest. Take my yoke upon you and learn from me, for I am gentle and humble in heart, and you will find rest for your souls. For my yoke is easy and my burden is light."

Scripture: Matthew 4:1-11

[1] Then Jesus was led by the Spirit into the wilderness to be tempted by the devil. [2] After fasting forty days and forty nights, he was hungry. [3] The tempter came to him and said, "If you are the Son of God, tell these stones to become bread." [4] Jesus answered, "It is written: 'Man shall not live on bread alone, but on every word that comes from the mouth of God.'"

[5] Then the devil took him to the holy city and had him stand on the highest point of the temple. [6] "If you are the Son of God," he said, "throw yourself down. For it is written:

"'He will command his angels concerning you,

and they will lift you up in their hands,

so that you will not strike your foot against a stone.'"

[7] Jesus answered him, "It is also written: 'Do not put the Lord your God to the test.'"

[8] Again, the devil took him to a very high mountain and showed him all the kingdoms of the world and their splendor. 9 "All this I will give you," he said, "if you will bow down and worship me." [10] Jesus said to him, "Away from me, Satan! For it is written: 'Worship the Lord your God, and serve him only.'"

[11] Then the devil left him, and angels came and attended him. (NIV)

Devotional: The Three Temptations

Jesus, as fully man and fully God, enlightened all of us.

He was the prototype of a sinless life. His example proves we too can be free from sin.

The Scriptures do not accredit Jesus's sinless life to his divine nature. He wasn't immune from sin because He left His "God mode" on. The writer of Hebrews tells us that, *"We do not have a high priest who is unable to empathize with our weaknesses, but we have one who has been tempted in every way, just as we are–yet he did not sin."*

Our struggle to live free from sin can distort our theology. We might struggle, but it should never redefine what Jesus made known. It's possible for us to live free from sin. We have been raised with Him, and we share in His divine nature.

Jesus showed us what's possible, and He empowered us with the necessary grace to follow His example. We need to draw on grace to empower us to live righteously.

It's important to remember Jesus was tempted. We can sometimes think temptation is sin, but it's not. Jesus was tempted, but without sin. It's what we do with temptation that matters. Jesus said satan was coming for him, but satan didn't have any claim on him.

Temptation is any opportunity to live inconsistent with truth.

Obedience is our opportunity to be the person God says we are.

Jesus was tempted in the wilderness by three major temptations. They followed the moment Jesus heard His identity from the Father. He heard, *"You are my beloved Son in whom I am well pleased."* He was affirmed in the unconditional love of His Father right before He was tested. The Spirit led Him into the wilderness because the temptations were testing the structural integrity of the Father's identity. Just who did Jesus believe He really was?

Jesus does not just give us an example for overcoming temptation. As the firstborn of new creation, His victory over temptation applies to all humanity. What happened to Jesus in the desert summarized every form of brokenness and compromise the rest of us would ever have to face.

Henri Nouwen helped me see how I was facing the same three temptations Jesus did in the wilderness. Like Jesus, we must face three false strategies for a life of fullness.

The three temptations we have to overcome are:

I am what I do.

I am what others think of me.

I am what I have.

When I am tempted to be defined by what I do, I try to prove my identity. I begin to measure my worth by what I did with today, and how I can do more tomorrow. I cover up my emotions by being overbusy. This temptation makes me nervous to slow down–if I fail, or do things wrong, my identity is thrown into jeopardy. But when I'm successful, I suddenly feel as if I am in control of the universe.

When I am tempted to be defined by what others think of me, I craft an image to get affection from people. I become consumed with how I appear, and I am crippled by the negative words of others. I begin doing things for the applause of people. This temptation pushes me to do something spectacular, and to make sure others know it.

When I am tempted to be defined by what I have, I try to accumulate things. These things can be experiences, or even an insatiable thirst for answers. I can begin to define my worth by my present measure of happiness, or by the larger questions I have figured out. I can be tempted to acquire whatever I think will give me security.

We can face any or all of these temptations. They're all opportunities to live inconsistent with the truth of our identity. Once we recognize them, we can say the same thing Jesus said about satan: he has no claim on us.

Question

How can you overcome one of the three temptations you're face?

_____

Prayer
Jesus, I repent for being defined by what I do. I repent for being defined by what others think of me. I repent for being defined by what I have. Jesus, those temptations have no say over my life. I abandon a life of falsehood, and I accept Your invitation into fullness. Jesus, I reconnect to the truth You have revealed about my life. Father, I am your son/daughter, with whom you are well-pleased. I am filled with unconditional love as I find my identity in the one who sits on the throne. It is in your name I pray. Amen.

Silence
2 minutes of sitting in silence being present to Jesus and yourself.

Presence

Holy Spirit lead me.
Holy Spirit sustain me.
Holy Spirit move through me.

Week One

Day 04

Presence

Jesus, be with me. My life is nothing without You. I long to be in Your Presence, where I find true rest. Wash over me with Your love, and cast out all of my fears. You're my safety. You're my hiding place. You're the one I run to. Everything is different when I am with You. As I rest here with You, overshadow me with Your loving Presence.

Silence

2 minutes of sitting in silence being present to Jesus and yourself.

Worship

Tell Jesus the place He has in your life and what He means to you.

Meditation

Matthew 11:28-30

Read it. Pray it. Ponder it.

"Come to me, all you who are weary and burdened, and I will give you rest. Take my yoke upon you and learn from me, for I am gentle and humble in heart, and you will find rest for your souls. For my yoke is easy and my burden is light."

Scripture: Matthew 11:28-30

[28] Come to me, all you who are weary and burdened, and I will give you rest. [29] Take my yoke upon you and learn from me, for I am gentle and humble in heart, and you will find rest for your souls. [30] For my yoke is easy and my burden is light. (NIV)

Devotional: Rest for the Soul

Our soul thirsts for God. If it doesn't get God, it will attempt to satisfy its thirst with other things. There is an ache within us. We long for love because we desire to be complete, and to rest.

Augustine of Hippo said, *"You have made us for yourself, and our hearts are restless, until they can find rest in you."*

God is not an ideology. He not a belief system. He is a person whose presence completes us. When we drink from the living water of being in His presence, we become satisfied. We stop covering up the ache of our need for Him. We settle into rest.

We don't find rest in principles–we find it by being with Him. I remember a season where my son was having such a struggle sleeping. He was roughly two years old, and he would wake up crying hard. I would come into his room, and the first words I'd say were, "I am here. I am here."

I didn't go into an intellectual explanation of why he didn't need to be scared. He wouldn't understand it anyway. He wasn't looking for answers. He was looking for my presence. My presence settled his heart. Presence satisfies what our soul needs, not necessarily what our head wants.

We cannot find rest by forecasting problems. We cannot find rest by answering all our doubts. We cannot find rest by eliminating questions. We find rest by allowing ourselves to trust that He is enough, and He will care for us.

The reason many of us don't find rest is because we don't seek it by being in His presence. Jesus offers us rest–a state of satisfied and settled living. He promises to take the heavy burdens and exchange them with His resounding peace. The promise of this exchange is connected to presence. He invites us to come to Him.

Jesus tells us to first come to him. It's in His presence that we truly gain progress.

We're addicted to pragmatism. We want something to solve our problems. We don't understand that rest can exist *even in the midst of problems.* The solution of being comforted by His presence doesn't necessarily eliminate our problem. Bishop Kallistos Ware calls this, *"trusting someone is there rather than something is true."*

It's faith in a person rather than an idea. Our soul will not experience the lightness–aka satisfaction–of relationship with Jesus unless we learn to receive comfort from Him instead of subverting our soul with activities to cover the aching.

It's scary to stop using our false strategies. It's almost easy to believe that worrying can be responsible. The truth is, trust is responsible. When we rely on His rest, we aren't being naive. Our soul thirsts for Him. This isn't going away. Let's learn to slow down enough to sense God. He is with us to satisfy us.

What's a lie you might be believing about God that keeps you from finding peace in God's presence during a tough season?

Prayer

Jesus, Introduce me to Your rest. Show me how You slept through the storm. Remind me of how You lived in the same chaos I face, but how You still knew peace. Jesus, I put my faith in You completely. I am blessed to experience Your Presence. I am certain that You cover my worry, and I am certain You conquer my burdens. Jesus, I embrace resting with You. It's in Your name I pray this. Amen

Silence

2 minutes of sitting in silence being present to Jesus and yourself.

Presence

Holy Spirit lead me.
Holy Spirit sustain me.
Holy Spirit move through me.

Week One

Day 05

Presence

Jesus, be with me. My life is nothing without You. I long to be in Your Presence, where I find true rest. Wash over me with Your love, and cast out all of my fears. You're my safety. You're my hiding place. You're the one I run to. Everything is different when I am with You. As I rest here with You, ⌣ shadow me with Your loving Presence.

Silence
2 minutes of sitting in silence being present to Jesus and yourself.

Worship
Tell Jesus the place He has in your life and what He means to you.

Meditation

Matthew 11:28-30

Read it. Pray it. Ponder it.

"Come to me, all you who are weary and burdened, and I will give you rest. Take my yoke upon you and learn from me, for I am gentle and humble in heart, and you will find rest for your souls. For my yoke is easy and my burden is light."

Scripture: Matthew 11:28-30
¹When Jesus spoke these words, he went out with his disciples across the brook Kidron, where there was a garden, which he and his disciples entered. ² Now Judas, who betrayed him, also knew the place, for Jesus often met there with his disciples. ³ So Judas, having procured a band of soldiers and some officers from the chief priests and the Pharisees, went there with lanterns and torches and weapons. ⁴ Then Jesus,

that would happen to him, came forward and
n, "Whom do you seek?" They answered him, [5]
zareth." Jesus said to them, "I am he." (ESV)

Devotional: Facing Pain

Jesus knew something about life most of us still need to learn.

Jesus was not blindsided by pain. Jesus never avoided pain to protect His own pure bliss—therefore, pain didn't catch Him off guard. Jesus has a great habit of going through things instead of around them. In the Garden of Gethsemane, Jesus came face-to-face with the cup of suffering before Him—and He submitted Himself to the will of His Father.

Jesus anticipated the pain ahead of Him.

Jesus knew all the things that would happen to Him, and He still came forward. He offered Himself up while knowing the unjust, nonsensical, and tragic events that would happen to Him. The impending pain didn't derail Jesus. He didn't strategize how to withdraw from the mob or avoid His approaching sacrifice. There was no way around it.

Avoiding pain wasn't up for discussion.

Jesus had to face His suffering head-on—but what we see in His example is still surprising: Suffering doesn't have to disfigure us or destroy us. Jesus provides a path through suffering. Jesus didn't die so that you and I would never have to experience pain or suffering. Instead, Jesus's suffering makes it possible for our pain to be transformed. Instead of living with open wounds, we follow the example of Jesus and become people who carry glorious scars.

Jesus kept his scars. He didn't hide them from us—but aren't still bleeding. His example proves God has a conclu sion and redemption for our pain.

Jesus's suffering is not a way for us to escape our own suffering. Jesus's endurance through suffering gives us the hope and confidence that we can remain whole. Suffering isn't a virtue—but it's possible to suffer with virtue.

This isn't a self-imposed suffering or an affliction Jesus solicited. Jesus wasn't self-destructive, and He wasn't negligent about His own self-care. Though we are called to follow His example, Jesus isn't asking us to take perverse pleasure in misery. His pain does not give us permission to despair. It empowers us to face despair with virtue.

Pain wasn't scary to Jesus because He never processed His pain in isolation. He abandoned Himself to the Father, knowing that He could entrust His well-being to the Father's care.

God is not the author of our pain—but He will use it. Jesus learned obedience through what He suffered. He was pressed and the virtue He carried was pressed out of Him. He suffered the stripes, and still carries the scars, for our healing. Jesus ends the cycle of pain by ending it within Himself. He doesn't perpetuate that pain by hurting others. When we suffer with virtue, we allow our pain to become a place of trust in God—which ultimately leads to healing. When we don't face our own pain, we can't heal the world.

Ignorance isn't bliss, it's a time-bomb for the soul. If Jesus would have avoided His own suffering, there would be no redemption for ours.

Question

Do you **have any current pain—or forecasted pain—**
you're avoiding, instead of learning to trust?

Prayer

God, I no longer pretend that pain doesn't exist in my life or
has no impact upon me. I refuse to let pain be a badge of
honor I wear—rather, I will begin to walk through my hurt,
knowing You walk right beside me. Thank You, Jesus, for
being a living example of One who doesn't avoid pain—but
instead goes through it. I ask that You give me insight on
what the next steps are to overcoming my pain—and that I
would feel Your Presence ever so closely through the process. Amen.

Silence

2 minutes of sitting in silence being present to Jesus and
yourself.

Presence

Holy Spirit lead me.
Holy Spirit sustain me.
Holy Spirit move through me.

Week One

Day 06

Presence

Jesus, be with me. My life is nothing without You. I long to
be in Your Presence, where I find true rest. Wash over me

with Your love, and cast out all of my fears. You're my safety. You're my hiding place. You're the one I run to. Everything is different when I am with You. As I rest here with You, over-shadow me with Your loving Presence.

Silence
2 minutes of sitting in silence being present to Jesus and yourself.

Worship
Tell Jesus the place He has in your life and what He means to you.

Meditation

Matthew 11:28-30

Read it. Pray it. Ponder it.

"Come to me, all you who are weary and burdened, and I will give you rest. Take my yoke upon you and learn from me, for I am gentle and humble in heart, and you will find rest for your souls. For my yoke is easy and my bur-den is light."

Scripture: Genesis 3:8
[8] Then the man and his wife heard the sound of the LORD God as he was walking in the garden in the cool of the day, and they hid from the LORD God among the trees of the garden. (NIV)

Devotional: Honest with God

We can never become whole without honesty.

We keep ourselves bound when we refuse to be honest with God. When we don't open our heart to Him. When we don't tell him we're angry about something happening to us. When we don't tell him about how we really feel.

We somehow think it's disrespectful to be honest. He is God, after all. We have this weird picture of Him being a temperamental parent—emotionally unavailable, and unable to handle the truth about how we're feeling.

We have it wrong. Honesty isn't disrespectful—it's an integral part of intimacy. And to our surprise, God is asking us, "How are you doing?" All the while, we're trying to put on a show to avoid offending Him with our emotions.

Jesus wants the real us. He doesn't heal egos—He heals people. We must begin to get comfortable sharing and defining how we're feeling with Jesus. This prepares us to receive His truth. It helps us out of destructive feelings like anger, hate, shame, and fear into productive emotions like peace, righteousness, joy, and love.

Honesty is the pathway toward positive feelings over negative feelings.

As we spend time with Jesus, we realize He is never absent in hard times. He does not ask us to deny how we've been impacted by something. If we deny our emotions in order to be with Jesus, we're actually lying to ourselves, and therefore never truly being present with Him. We give Him a false self.

We spend our attention covering reality, rather than offering it to Him.

He wants to know you.

He is ready to listen.

He is emotionally available.

God knows your life, but He is like a good friend who wants to be told about your life. We have to let the truth that *"God is love"* guide how we interact with Him. Love bears all things. Love wants to know how you're doing on the inside. When we read that love bears all things and endures all things, it must therefore be true about the way God treats us. He will subject Himself to us in order to heal us. He will listen to what He already knows—because when we process, we heal.

Jesus often asked the unmistakably sick what they wanted from Him. Their pain was apparent but Jesus' invitation for them was to own growth by vocalizing their desire in life. It's the same for our emotions. As we share our emotional reality in God's presence, He helps us describe and name the feelings we've been denying. God cannot help us process what we are unwilling to acknowledge.

If we hide this information about ourselves, the relationship remains distant. Unless we move toward confession, we may never get free. If the blind man said "I am fine," he would have left Jesus blind and not healed.

Sometimes God will reveal our emotions to us—but our failure to be honest about them makes it so hard to receive His help. God will tell us we're angry, but if we refuse to acknowledge the anger we will stay trapped within its prison. We're afraid that if we agree with God, it means we're horrible people. God simply is the faithful friend who wounds us by making us aware of what's really going on inside of us. It takes a willingness to be honest with God to accept what God shows us.

God even endures when our emotions are directed at Him. The Bible has many accounts of faithful people who were willing to question God and confront Him with the real condition of their heart.

Honesty doesn't always mean accuracy. If we're honest with God, it doesn't mean we're right. It means we have enough connection to endure when we misunderstand His feedback—and we have enough trust to know He will not misunderstand us. He listens to us and corrects us. But God can't prescribe the right solution when we give him lies about our emotions.

Trust His love will always be bigger than your honesty. Trust He will hold you in the middle of your process. Refuse to hide from God.

Jesus was troubled and wept but wasn't hopeless. Our emotions when brought to God are not distractions but pathways for Him to secure us. We have to be honest about what we're feeling or our self numbing, rather than our feelings themselves, will cause hopelessness.

Question

What are you angry about today? Sad about? Ashamed about? Hurt about?

Prayer

God, I give myself over to You. All of me. All of my emotions—known and unknown. Thank You for loving me and seeing me through the lens of your love, no matter what I am going through. I trust that You will not leave me in my pain, confusion, or shame. I ask that you give me insight about what is going on inside of me, and give me the strength to be honest about it. Guide me through this new journey of being vulnerable with you—and bring me to deeper levels of honesty with You, myself, and others. Amen.

Silence

2 minutes of sitting in silence being present to Jesus and yourself.

Presence

Holy Spirit lead me.
Holy Spirit sustain me.
Holy Spirit move through me.

Week One

Day 07

Presence

Jesus, be with me. My life is nothing without You. I long to be in Your Presence, where I find true rest. Wash over me with Your love, and cast out all of my fears. You're my safety. You're my hiding place. You're the one I run to. Everything is different when I am with You. As I rest here with You, overshadow me with Your loving Presence.

Silence

2 minutes of sitting in silence being present to Jesus and yourself.

Worship

Tell Jesus the place He has in your life and what He means to you.

Psalm of the week **23**

Matthew **7**

Matthew 11:28-30

Read it. Pray it. Ponder it.

"Come to me, all you who are weary and burdened, and I will give you rest. Take my yoke upon you and learn from me, for I am gentle and humble in heart, and you will find rest for your souls. For my yoke is easy and my burden is light."

Scripture: Matthew 3:17

[17] "This is my beloved Son in whom I am well pleased." (NASB)

Devotional: The Father's Pleasure

If we're first motivated by the opinions of others, and if we're swayed by their affections, we will craft a certain image of ourselves to gain their affirmation. But it's possible to live free from this kind of false identity.

We absolutely can be our truest selves, regardless of whether or not it pleases those around us. It is actually possible to live uncontrolled by the opinions of others. Even the opinions that make you want to crawl right back into the crafted image of yourself.

God offers us an anchor to live free from the fear of man.

The fear of man is when we consult people about our worth, value, and acceptance before we seek those things from God. This fear locks us into working for their love–a love that is conditional at best. A love that includes the price tag of their conditional approval.

But it's scary standing out.

Not sticking with the crowd can feel vulnerable. You even feel open for attack. The world can seem like a sea of sameness, where everyone is drowning in the fear of being different. Society often seems like a giant cannibal, trying to keep the status quo by eating parts of itself.

The fear of man has crippled and taken out so many of us. Some of us never take the first step towards our dreams, because we're afraid of what "they" will think of us. Life presents us with an inescapable temptation to be inauthentic. Whether we're loud, quiet, introverted, or extroverted, being ourselves is a real battle. The fear of man will control us as long as we find our self-worth in the words of others.

The power to change is available to those who dare to stand out. Standing out requires a pillar to hold us. We need a stabilizer for our identity, or we will never hold fast to who we are, or use our voice for change. If we don't find this anchor, then hiding our true selves will become our 9-5 job.

God offers us the same anchor He offered to Jesus.

When Jesus was about thirty years old, He went public with His ministry. We all know the moment you go public, you open yourself up to the opinions, criticisms, and misunderstandings of others. Standing out can make you look like a

McDonald's Big Mac to a hungry crowd. Jesus had opportunities to hide and please others while living on earth. He had to face this temptation or he wouldn't have been fully human. Jesus could have lived for the pleasures of the crowd, but He didn't–because He had something so much better than their opinion.

As Jesus went into the public eye, He heard a voice from His Father in Heaven saying, "This is My beloved Son in whom I am well-pleased." This truth anchored Him. We know it did because He died on the Cross for a choice that didn't please the crowd.

Jesus was massively misunderstood in His life. He was called things that were flat-out lies. People misunderstood and misrepresented His message. Nonetheless, He never betrayed Himself.

He denied the praises of man.

Jesus didn't need the praises of others, because He had the pleasure of His Father. He didn't fear rejection from the world, because He knew He was accepted by God. When you know you're accepted by God, no one else can reject you.

Crowds would surround Jesus regularly. Some would sing His praises, and others would try to kill Him. Either way, the crowd didn't influence Him. The biblical writers described Jesus as withdrawing from the crowd to pray. He would leave not because He feared them, but because He was actually called to minister to them. Simply put, Jesus wouldn't let them control Him.

If you cannot leave the crowd, then you're not ready to minister to the crowd.

Only when you're anchored in God's acceptance will you have the power to leave the crowd. We will fear the rejection of others when we are uncertain of our acceptance. We will hide our true voice when the love we get from people feels more real than the love we receive from God.

However, when we know we're accepted by God, the power to change the world is in our hands. God's acceptance gives us permission. It invites us to never hide again.

Question

Do you hide any part of you (good or bad) because you're afraid of what others will think about you?

_____

Prayer

God, Thank You for making me uniquely set apart. Continue to reveal when I hide my true self from others because of fear. I pray You give me courage, like Jesus, to speak when You've asked me to speak, and to walk away from the crowd when You've asked me to withdraw. I refuse to hide because You, God, are my Anchor. Amen.

Silence

2 minutes of sitting in silence being present to Jesus and yourself.

Presence

Holy Spirit lead me.
Holy Spirit sustain me.
Holy Spirit move through me.

Week
Two

Presence

Jesus, You're here with me. My heart is glad, and full of joy in your Presence. I belong here. The world might misunderstand me, but You understand me. You see me and know me. Speak to me like a man speaks to a friend. I'll let go of everything so I can be here with You. You're what holds me together.

Silence

2 minutes of sitting in silence being present to Jesus and yourself.

Worship

Tell Jesus the place He has in your life and what He means to you.

Psalm of the week **63**

Matthew **8**

Meditation

1 Corinthians 13:4-7

Read it. Pray it. Ponder it.

Love is patient and kind; love does not envy or boast; it is not arrogant or rude. It does not insist on its own way; it is not irritable or resentful; 6 it does not rejoice at wrongdoing, but rejoices with the truth. Love bears all things, believes all things, hopes all things, endures all things.

Scripture: Luke 10: 38-42

[38] Now as they went on their way, Jesus entered a village. And a woman named Martha welcomed him into her house. [39] And she had a sister called Mary, who sat at the Lord's feet and listened to his teaching. [40] But Martha was distracted with much serving. And she went up to him and said, "Lord, do you not care that my sister has left me to serve alone? Tell her then to help me." [41] But the Lord answered her, "Martha, Martha, you are anxious and troubled about many things, [42] but one thing is necessary. Mary has chosen the good portion, which will not be taken away from her." (ESV)

Devotional: Mary and Martha

I've heard people say we need to have the attitudes of both Mary and Martha. They say it as an attempt to stop people from being disorganized, lazy and unwilling to serve. The problem is that Jesus didn't endorse both of their mentalities.

Jesus confronts how Martha is covering up her life.

Jesus reveals Martha to herself through Mary. Martha realizes she's only serving to cover up her anxiety. Martha isn't a productive person. Instead, she is a person that is busy doing things to avoid the anxiety she has within herself. I am sure there are many things for Mary to do, but she knows one thing is necessary–and that one thing is to take the opportunity to be intimate with Jesus.

We need to be reminded that productivity *for* God does not trump intimacy *with* God.

Jesus sees through the facade and recognizes there's something deeper going on in Martha's heart. Martha can't recognize her own broken motives. She tries to cover up her anxiety by doing all the "right things", and then complains when people are not doing what she thinks is necessary. She judges her sister for choosing to sit at Jesus's feet, instead of helping her with all the serving.

We often sacrifice our time with God to get things done in life. We can tell ourselves, "I don't have time to spend with God–there's too much to be done." We're worried our life will fall apart if we stop to be with Jesus.

We don't feel safe enough to stop. We don't trust that being with Jesus will make us more productive in the long run. We're addicted to the demands of our day.

It's popular to be busy.

We don't see the flaws in overworking ourselves. Yet, if we give our time to Jesus, He will heal the anxiety which is driving our work–ultimately allowing our work to flourish. There will always be things I can accomplish with my limited attention. There will always be people I could serve. There are always problems to solve. There are always ways to cover up my anxiety with more activity.

Jesus invites us to let all that go, and be with him.

We all know that this is the only thing which will really cure our anxiety. Jesus gives us peace that puts an end to our overworking, which frees us to do what He is asking us to do in life.

Be with Him.

Do you find that you cover up your feelings with doing things, instead of addressing those feelings in His presence?

Prayer

Jesus, I come to sit at Your feet. Please still my heart, mind, and hands. Jesus, I repent for hiding behind my work. I repent for allowing the world's standards of busyness to steal away my time with You. I ask that You show me where I am choosing work above relationship today. I come now to sit at your feet like Mary did. Ready to breathe in your peace and Presence. Thank You for grace and wisdom. I love you, Abba. Amen.

Silence

2 minutes of sitting in silence being present to Jesus and yourself.

Presence

Holy Spirit lead me.
Holy Spirit sustain me.
Holy Spirit move through me.

Week Two

Day 09

Presence

Jesus, You're here with me. My heart is glad, and full of joy in your Presence. I belong here. The world might misunderstand me, but You understand me. You see me and know me. Speak to me like a man speaks to a friend. I'll let go of everything so I can be here with You. You're what holds me together.

Silence

2 minutes of sitting in silence being present to Jesus and yourself.

Worship

Tell Jesus the place He has in your life and what He means to you.

Psalm of the week **63**

Matthew 9

Love is patient and kind; love does not envy or boast; it is not arrogant or rude. It does not insist on its own way; it is not irritable or resentful; 6 it does not rejoice at wrongdoing, but rejoices with the truth. Love bears all things, believes all things, hopes all things, endures all things.

Scripture: Philippians 3:8-10

8 Indeed, I count everything as loss because of the surpassing worth of knowing Christ Jesus my Lord. For his sake I have suffered the loss of all things and count them as rubbish, in order that I may gain 9 Christ and be found in him, not having a righteousness of my own that comes from the law, but that which comes through faith in Christ, the righteousness from God that depends on faith—10 that I may know him. (ESV)

Devotional: Count All As Loss

I don't need to have all the answers before I cultivate the inner impulse to love God. Love transcends everything.

My love for Him is supported by theological exploration–but it doesn't rest there. Ironing out all the truth about God does not necessarily make me closer to Him. The journey into love is not usually by intellectual assent, but by the willingness to abandon myself in His presence.

John Wesley said, *"Orthodoxy, or right opinion, is at best, a very slender part of religion...There may be a right opinion of God without either love or one right temper toward Him. Satan is proof of this."*

We might be able to answer our theological questions without increasing our desire to be with Jesus. Our theological "rightness" provides a sense of inner relief that masquerades as intimacy. I might be able to tell you all the facts about my wife, but that doesn't mean I am in a good relationship with her.

We cannot place anything over being in love with Him.

Our love for God animates and sustains everything we value. We can delight in all kinds of studies and ministry, but we cannot neglect the opportunities we have to show Him our affection. We cannot be casual about worshiping Him.

We may have healthy pursuits, but they must be secondary.

We absolutely should pursue personal transformation.

We should engage with spiritual practices that form us.

We ought to discover more about our emotional health, and become more stable and mature in our conduct.

We must learn how to love those around us better.

But our dreams and passions can distract us from simply loving Him. It's only when God is the chief desire of our hearts that we may prosper in every other desire.

It is impossible to gain traction in godliness or any endeavor without first attending to God's supreme place above the spectrum of our affections. It is crucial to pay attention to our desire–or lack of desire–for Him. If our love is fading, then our life is disordered. We have made secondary things primary. Is His surpassing worth changing my values until I'd intuitively count everything as loss for the sake of knowing Him more? Is He that captivating to me? Do I dream to be overcome by His love? Do I thirst to be in His presence?

I open myself to God's love for me and, in turn, love Him more. I do this as the mainspring of my life. It's not something I graduate from or mature out of. This sort of pursuit must be the transcendent value of my life. I must be willing to want Him over anything else. There is no shame in acknowledging my lack of desire for God–nor is there any benefit in pretending to want God just for the sake of fulfilling the expectations of my religious ego. We're designed to have a love for God and a thirst for His presence–and yet it must be cultivated.

Jesus is always ready to show you how a day with Him is better than a thousand elsewhere. The inner impulse to love God is first a choice I make: I must find myself in the arms of a Father who holds me so well.

Counting everything else as loss isn't supposed to be impressive or complicated. It's simple: I only seek to be with Him.

Have certain dreams (even God-given dreams) become a distraction from simply loving God?

Prayer

Jesus, I love You. I love You, not for what You can give, but because of who You are–because You are the one thing in my life that deserves all my attention and affection. The fullness of life is not found in the things I can attain; it is found in You. I count it all as loss if I cannot have You. No person, no monetary value, no achievement can fill the space in my heart that belongs to You. I ask for a deeper awareness of Your Presence today. Amen.

Silence

2 minutes of sitting in silence being present to Jesus and yourself.

Presence

Holy Spirit lead me.
Holy Spirit sustain me.
Holy Spirit move through me.

Week Two

Day 10

Presence

Jesus, You're here with me. My heart is glad, and full of joy in your Presence. I belong here. The world might misunderstand me, but You understand me. You see me and know me. Speak to me like a man speaks to a friend. I'll let go of everything so I can be here with You. You're what holds me together.

Silence

2 minutes of sitting in silence being present to Jesus and yourself.

Worship

Tell Jesus the place He has in your life and what He means to you.

Meditation

1 Corinthians 13:4-7

Read it. Pray it. Ponder it.

Love is patient and kind; love does not envy or boast; it is not arrogant or rude. It does not insist on its own way; it is not irritable or resentful; 6 it does not rejoice at wrongdoing, but rejoices with the truth. Love bears all things, believes all things, hopes all things, endures all things.

Scripture: Acts 1:8

8 "You will receive power when the Holy Spirit comes on you; and you will be my witnesses in Jerusalem, and in all Judea and Samaria, and to the ends of the earth". (NIV)

Devotional: Waiting on the Spirit

Jesus will take us places we would never dream of going, and He will empower us to do things beyond what we ever thought we could do. He is wild about sharing His capabilities with us. He doesn't make us dependent upon our natural talents. He provides us with the very same Spirit that empowered Him.

You and I need the Spirit.

We need the Spirit first for ourselves, and second for each other.

After Jesus's resurrection, He commissions His disciples to go to the world with the message of God's availability of healing. They're told they will cross every social, ethnic, and geographic barrier–but before they go, they must wait.

Waiting precedes going.

Jesus told His disciples to wait for the Holy Spirit to come upon them. This waiting was a posture of surrender, not just a pause in work. Surrender is a posture of lifelong dependency. Surrender is the secret to our effectiveness.

Why?

If He is sharing His capabilities with us, we need the same Spirit that empowered Him. We cannot do what God has sent us out to do without His Spirit. If we think we can be effective without mirroring Jesus's dependency on the Spirit, then we're at best, naive–and at worst, deceived.

Jesus asked His disciples to wait for the Spirit. He seemed to think they needed power to be His witnesses. The outpouring at Pentecost, then, is the empowering dimension of the Spirit's work in our lives. It's different than the work of the Spirit for salvation. We cannot know Christ without the Spirit, but we can attempt to do the work of ministry without the Spirit. The Pentecost narrative is the transfer of the charismatic dimension of the Spirit from Jesus to His disciples.

Up to this point, the disciples had seen some remarkable things–but they couldn't rush onto the next thing, because they needed to receive something new. They needed the Holy Spirit in a dimension they had yet to experience. The power of the Spirit was non-negotiable for Jesus, and so it must also be for us.

Our vision isn't enough.

Our experience level isn't enough.

Our training isn't enough.

I love how severe the revivalist John G. Lake was, in describing his need for more of the Spirit. He said, *"But my heart was crying for deliverance; my soul had come to the place where I had vomited up dependence on man."*

We must have a posture of waiting for the Spirit. This is a continual, abiding surrender to the Spirit. A regular openness that displaces overdependence on man.

In our day, we can create a great strategy to build our community–but without the power of the Spirit, we're just gathering people. We can learn to grow our influence–and it's true that influence will gather people–but influence doesn't break bondages. It can't heal the sick or raise the dead. Formulas might get our churches full, but our people won't be full of the Spirit.

You might have everything you think you need to be successful, but without the Spirit you have nothing. He is indispensable, and our surrender to Him is non-negotiable. If we don't plan to be open to the Spirit, we're closed. There's no neutral ground.

Even the smallest amount of indifference is a resistance to the Spirit. He will actively try to overcome your limits, but He will ultimately respect your decision—leaving you to your own callousness, and to the exhaustion of your own human effort.

Pentecost isn't a moment, but a posture. We wait to give the Spirit the place that matters most. The first place. We will not go until we are saturated in the power of the Spirit.

Question

What part of you needs to die in order to begin waiting on the Spirit in your life?

_____

Prayer
Jesus, I am here in the now moments contending for Your full power. I rid myself of any indifference and I repent for any resistance. I am after Your Spirit and Your Spirit alone. Jesus, my strategies are not enough, my training is not enough, my negotiating is not enough. Jesus, only Your Spirit will be enough. I want Your Spirit. Jesus, I lean into Your fullness with complete grace. I am made new by Your unceasing love. It is in Your name that I pray this again and again. Amen.

Silence
2 minutes of sitting in silence being present to Jesus and yourself.

Presence
Holy Spirit lead me.
Holy Spirit sustain me.
Holy Spirit move through me.

Presence

Jesus, You're here with me. My heart is glad, and full of joy in your Presence. I belong here. The world might misunderstand me, but You understand me. You see me and know me. Speak to me like a man speaks to a friend. I'll let go of everything so I can be here with You. You're what holds me together.

Silence

2 minutes of sitting in silence being present to Jesus and yourself.

Worship

Tell Jesus the place He has in your life and what He means to you.

Meditation

1 Corinthians 13:4–7

Read it. Pray it. Ponder it.

Psalm of the week **63**

Matthew **11**

Love is patient and kind; love does not envy or boast; it is not arrogant or rude. It does not insist on its own way; it is not irritable or resentful; 6 it does not rejoice at wrongdoing, but rejoices with the truth. Love bears all things, believes all things, hopes all things, endures all things.

Scripture: Romans 6:4-11

⁴ We were therefore buried with him through baptism into death in order that, just as Christ was raised from the dead through the glory of the Father, we too may live a new life. ⁵ For if we have been united with him in a death like his, we will certainly also be united with him in a resurrection like his. ⁶ For we know that our old self was crucified with him so that the body ruled by sin might be done away with, that we should no longer be slaves to sin—⁷ because anyone who has died has been set free from sin.

⁸ Now if we died with Christ, we believe that we will also live with him. ⁹ For we know that since Christ was raised from the dead, he cannot die again; death no longer has mastery over him. ¹⁰ The death he died, he died to sin once for all; but the life he lives, he lives to God.

¹¹ In the same way, count yourselves dead to sin but alive to God in Christ Jesus. (NIV)

Devotional: New Self

Jesus has done something unmistakable and irreversible. The world can never go back to the way it was before God took on flesh. The scope of what He has done is so deep and wide that it merits being called a new creation.

The finished work of Jesus' death and resurrection is sufficient for the total and complete renewal of all things. His victory lacks nothing and requires no supplements. Christ is enough for the human condition to be healed of all its brokenness.

The depth of the anticipated transformation for us is, honestly, scandalous. It's almost unbelievable. We are called to consider our old fragmented life as no longer existent. Our new life now mirrors Christ's very own life. Every part of our being has been touched by the work of Jesus—and transformation unfolds as we renew our mind to the truth of Jesus' work.

This means we undermine the Cross by claiming we're still sinners who are inclined toward doing evil. When we see how Christ has transformed our lives, we stop believing our default setting is to sin. We stop believing our identity is based on our past. We stop believing our addictions will bind us forever.

Christ is enough or He isn't enough. There's never "almost enough" in Christ.

We've been included in Christ's death, and we've been included in His resurrection. We don't take any of our old life with us up from the burial of baptism. We leave it behind and embrace the new self. This is a complete overhaul of our life. It means that we have a new identity with all new soul cravings, attitudes, and behaviors.

Jesus isn't asking us to manage our old life. He is asking to replace it entirely.

When Jesus replaces our old life with His life, we are set free from our sin and from its power. This means you and I are no longer running on the effects of sin or fueled by it. We are clean. You're no longer a sinner with a default setting to sin. You're righteous like Christ, and you have a default setting to love God. You're dead to sin and alive to God.

We might still sin because, according to Paul, we are still

working out our salvation. This means we grow in the practice of letting Jesus have an unhindered way with us. It's about living consistent with our identity by recognizing the lies we still live under. We might have a new life, but the enemy is still a liar, and we might have listened to him for a long time.

We have to retrain our entire being according to the truth of Christ's transformation.

My wife gave me the best way to picture this reality, and it involves white shoes. We all know what it's like to wear a brand new pair of white shoes. We spot the first speck of dirt and, over time, we tolerate it. When Christ makes us clean, it's like we're given a brand new pair of white shoes, and the conviction of the Spirit helps recognize the first spot of dirt. We only clean the dirt when we recognize the standard has changed.

We now spot the dirt and say "This doesn't belong, because I am clean." It's only when we tolerate the dirt long enough–forgetting our own transformation–that we stop being convicted of our newness. We start talking like we're just dirty, instead of asking to be refreshed.

We're new people in Christ. We're not "kind of" new, but an entirely new person. Life is now about living consistent with the sufficient work of Jesus in us.

Question

Are there any marks of dirt in my life that I have grown accustomed to?

Prayer

Jesus, You are the one I love. You have buried my old ways and raised me up in Your goodness. You have broken me free from the lifestyle of sin, and welcomed me fully into a new life. Jesus, Your name is higher than any other—and that is the name I will exalt. I have been made new. Jesus, I am so thankful for Your transforming love. Jesus, guide me to live out of my new self. Amen.

Silence

2 minutes of sitting in silence being present to Jesus and yourself.

Presence

Holy Spirit lead me.
Holy Spirit sustain me.
Holy Spirit move through me.

Week Two

Day 12

Presence

Jesus, You're here with me. My heart is glad, and full of joy in your Presence. I belong here. The world might misunderstand me, but You understand me. You see me and know me. Speak to me like a man speaks to a friend. I'll let go of everything so I can be here with You. You're what holds me together.

Silence

2 minutes of sitting in silence being present to Jesus and yourself.

Worship

Tell Jesus the place He has in your life and what He means to you.

1 Corinthians 13:4-7

Read it. Pray it. Ponder it.

Love is patient and kind; love does not envy or boast; it is not arrogant or rude. It does not insist on its own way; it is not irritable or resentful; it does not rejoice at wrongdoing, but rejoices with the truth. Love bears all things, believes all things, hopes all things, endures all things.

Scripture: Luke 9:23-25

23 If anyone desires to come after Me, let him deny himself, and take up his cross daily, and follow Me. 25 For whoever desires to save his life will lose it, but whoever loses his life for My sake will save it. 25 For what profit is it to a man if he gains the whole world, and is himself destroyed or lost? (NKJV)

Devotional: Death to Self

The great German pastor and theologian Dietrich Bonhoeffer once said, *"When Christ calls a man, he bids him come and die."*

Dietrich was simply echoing the words of Jesus. We will never embody Jesus's life without understanding our call to join ourselves to Christ's death. A disciple's invitation is to lose their life in order to find it.

We're meant to be like a grain of wheat. A seed must first fall to the ground before it can bring forth produce. The pattern of Christlikeness is death and resurrection. God requires us to let go in order to embody His life. We let go of any attitude, behavior, or feeling found in our old self that was constructed upon a lie about God or our own identity in Christ.

Death to self isn't to be confused with the death of self. Jesus does not condone self-hatred. If anything, Jesus elevates our worth beyond what we could ever claim or measure! But self-denial and self-rejection are two different things.

An example of self-rejection would be, "I'm disgusting and worthless." An example of death to self would be, "I deeply want to fight back with my words, but I recognize that I don't have to follow that instinct anymore." It's letting go of a lesser life in order for your new life in Christ to emerge.

Dallas Willard said, *"One problem that has hindered this teaching in the past is that those presenting it have not carefully drawn the distinction between death to and death of self. As a result, people view death to self as if it means getting rid of yourself. That is not at all what it involves. You were not put here on earth to get rid of yourself. You were put here to be a self, and to live fully as a self. The worth of the self—your self—is inestimable, and God's intent for you is that you become a fully realized self as you make the grace-fueled movement from the old self to the new."*

This isn't about becoming morbid and stoic, constantly denying yourself of joy. The book of Hebrews tells us that Jesus actually endured the cross for joy. Death to self is about finding your life, not rejecting it. And we find our life by surrendering our right to live for ourselves.

When we lay down our instinctive selfishness, He begins to

direct us. Our old impulses and destructive habits are just as dead as our independence is. When we do not die to ourselves, we try to justify our old patterns. It's the only way we can defend ourselves and prove our best intentions. But this only protects our dysfunctions–and we lose our soul in exchange for false security.

We end up living as our old self, trusting ourselves over God. We remain discontent and restless, and we struggle to let God guide us.

Some of us continue to fight for applause, because we cannot live without the approval of people.

Some of us continue to vent our anger, trying to control others.

Some of us continue to hide our sin because we fear rejection.

Some of us continue to avoid prayer because it's too much of a sacrifice.

Jesus beckons us to die to whatever is trying to keep that alive, so that we can truly be born again. *Jesus helps us become self-aware.* He helps us observe and understand why we're doing things. He creates this opportunity for self-awareness, so that whatever we observe we can also deny a place of influence. Jesus begins to show us to ourselves so that He might rescue us from ourselves. This is painful because it feels like we're dying. It will be painful at first to forgive someone who hurt us rather than hurt them back. But, over time, this death to self will cause a new life to emerge–one that forgives others as easily as it hurt others before. When we die to ourselves, we initially fight the feeling that our sense of justice is being violated. We also have to let go of feeling right and our other habitual responses.

It's possible to live content, satisfied, and full of joy without always getting what we want in life. God put two trees in the garden to show it's possible to have a "no" from God and still live fulfilled. God will do a better job leading us if we trust Him by honoring the limits God places in front of us. Limits aren't wrong–they're life-giving. God has boundaries for our well-being to keep us from living out of our old, broken sense of self.

When we deny our old self, we are essentially shutting the door on trusting ourselves. We no longer try to meet all our own needs. This feels like death because we're used to finding peace by controlling things. We have to release our impulse to protect our reputation, image, security or feelings. We must retrain our habits to stop reaching for the false security our possessions afford to us. We do this so the new self can emerge. But we are not just stopping something. We're giving room for what's true about Christ to be expressed through us.

We crucify the self that needs to die so the life Christ embodied can be our own. When you go to the cross to die to yourself, you end up finding Jesus there. He is waiting to lead you through death and into resurrection. Jesus beckons us to die because He wants to bury our old self and all its false desires to give us an eternally fulfilling life.

He asks us to die to hiding our emotions.

He asks us to die to controlling others with fear or anger.

He asks us to die to seeking the approval of others.

He asks us to die to finding our value in things.

He asks us to die to whatever isn't inside the heart of Jesus.

Question

What are two specific things God is asking to die in you?

_____

Prayer

Jesus, You know me through and through. Your invitation to die to my old self is not a burden, but my privilege as a follower of Yours. You have already given me the grace to pick up my cross and deny myself, because Your protective, fulfilling love finds me there. I ask that you would continue to show me the areas that still need to die, and give me the courage to walk that out. Amen.

Silence

2 minutes of sitting in silence being present to Jesus and yourself.

Presence

Holy Spirit lead me.
Holy Spirit sustain me.
Holy Spirit move through me.

Week Two
_____
Day 13

Presence

Jesus, You're here with me. My heart is glad, and full of joy in your Presence. I belong here. The world might misunderstand me, but You understand me. You see me and know me. Speak to me like a man speaks to a friend. I'll let go of everything so I can be here with You. You're what holds me together.

Silence
2 minutes of sitting in silence being present to Jesus and yourself.

Worship
Tell Jesus the place He has in your life and what He means to you.

Meditation

1 Corinthians 13:4-7
Read it. Pray it. Ponder it.

Love is patient and kind; love does not envy or boast; it is not arrogant or rude. It does not insist on its own way; it is not irritable or resentful; it does not rejoice at wrongdoing, but rejoices with the truth. Love bears all things, believes all things, hopes all things, endures all things.

Scripture: Psalm 63:1
¹O God, You are my God; Early will I seek You; My soul thirsts for You; My flesh longs for You In a dry and thirsty land Where there is no water. (NKJV)

Devotional: Thirst After God
Nothing is impossible with God, but there's absolutely something He is unwilling to do. He will not be alone. He wants

to be with us. God has committed to being more than a gift -giver. He is not content with simply blessing us. He wants to give us Himself.

The great goal of our life is to love God. You cannot find a better purpose. The best thing I could ever do with my time is to reflect the love He gives right back to Him. There's a way of knowing Jesus that knows how wise it is to pour a full year's wages worth of perfume upon His feet. We can know Him in such a ravishing way that our soul finds nothing comparable to Him.

Jesus is captivating unless we're deceived.

Once He makes Himself known to us, our hearts begin to burn for Him. We're drawn in by His affection and, in turn, He causes a radical love for Him to erupt within us.

We become discontent with our ideas about Him. We cannot talk about Him like He isn't in the room anymore. We stop the religious jargon, because those words are no longer sufficient to describe a person we know beyond the rhythms of our rituals. We're longing to continually taste and see Him. We can no longer tolerate secondhand information from those who've been face-to-face with Him. We're no longer content to remain in the audience of other people's stories— we must experience Him for ourselves.

A.W Tozer said, "*Whoever seeks God as a means toward desired ends will not find God. God will not be one of many treasures. His mercy and grace are infinite, and His patient understanding is beyond measure. But He will not aid men in selfish striving after personal gain. If we love God as much as we should, surely we cannot dream of a loved object be-*

yond Him that He might help us to obtain!"

Our love should place Him upon the throne of our heart unchallenged. The great unction to seek Him is the very purpose of all spiritual revivals. God is not aching for people to be busy with revival meetings. He is aching for people to be radically in love with Him.

He is drawing all of us unto Himself, to ignite a life of following after Him.

A revival is when the Spirit comes upon the slumbering consciousness of men, with such unmistakable nearness, that His presence leads us to abandon all pursuits but the pursuit of Him. We begin to hunger to speak to God as a man speaks to a friend; face-to-face.

Those who cultivate this hunger for God can even experience it like the body hungers for food. And Christ has promised we will not be left empty. God is not a tease. He doesn't cause us to hunger for what He never intended to satisfy. He only asks us to remain in pursuit long enough to move beyond facts about Him–and into the vulnerability of knowing Him intimately.

He only asks us to remain in pursuit long enough to be reshaped by our growing hunger for Him. He only allows your hunger and thirst to grow to the measure of His impending infilling. But He promised that the hungry will be filled.

Question

Have you settled in your life with God in an area where He is inviting you into something deeper?

Prayer

God, I wake up to thoughts of your matchlessness. My heart, mind, and soul longs for Your wondrous ways. I find refuge in Your majesty. God, I will seek You with total abandonment. I have searched the things of this world, and none measure up. I am thirsting after Your power and Your glory. God, my soul shall be satisfied by You alone—and my mouth shall proclaim Your truths. And when I am encountered by You, I will never pull away. God, You are the one that I need. It is in your name I pray. Amen.

Silence

2 minutes of sitting in silence being present to Jesus and yourself.

Presence

Holy Spirit lead me.
Holy Spirit sustain me.
Holy Spirit move through me.

Week Two

Day 14

Presence

Jesus, You're here with me. My heart is glad, and full of joy in your Presence. I belong here. The world might misunderstand me, but You understand me. You see me and know me. Speak to me like a man speaks to a friend. I'll let go of everything so I can be here with You. You're what holds me together.

Silence

2 minutes of sitting in silence being present to Jesus and yourself.

Worship

Tell Jesus the place He has in your life and what He means to you.

1 Corinthians 13:4-7

Read it. Pray it. Ponder it.

Love is patient and kind; love does not envy or boast; it is not arrogant or rude. It does not insist on its own way; it is not irritable or resentful; it does not rejoice at wrongdoing, but rejoices with the truth. Love bears all things, believes all things, hopes all things, endures all things.

Scripture: Proverbs 4:23

23 "Above all else, guard your heart, for everything you do flows from it." (NIV)

Devotional: Well-Kept Heart

An overlooked quality of Jesus is His restraint. Jesus intentionally limited Himself. I am not talking about Jesus limiting Himself from His full capacity as God. I am talking about His surrendered self–a self that isn't controlled by outside influences. Jesus is incredibly self-controlled. This has to do with Jesus's inner core–the center of Jesus's being and motivation.

Jesus has a well-kept heart.

What does that mean? Jesus was a person who responded

to situations in ways that were good and right. He resisted what needed resisting, and He embraced what needed embracing. He didn't find Himself out of control. Rather, all his human capacities (His thoughts, emotions, body, and interactions with others) cooperated with His choice to live in godliness. He had a well-kept heart.

What is the heart?

Dallas Willard taught, "*The heart is the center or core of the human being, and the part to which every other component of the self owes its proper functioning.*" We have a spiritual reality inside of us that has the power to initiate, direct, and create. This can also be referred to as the will. The heart and will can, at times, be interchangeable terms.

We begin to keep our heart when our will is surrendered to God's will. When we turn over the power to direct ourselves by trusting in God, our heart becomes tender and safe. We discover that God does not want to micromanage our lives–He wants to teach us how to use our freedom.. We surprisingly feel self-controlled because our surrendered will transforms into an empowered will.

When we don't surrender our will to God, we then direct our lives without the help of the Holy Spirit.

The will is capable of directing the interplay of our entire being. When we learn how to keep our heart like Jesus did, we begin to have a healthy cooperation between what we think, what we feel, what we habitually do, and how we relate to others. We can choose the thoughts that renew us over the thoughts that destroy us. We can engage with our emotions to understand the reason for those emotions. We can retrain our body away from the slavery of ingrained, destructive habits. But our will alone can never change a person. We need our will to be empowered by the Spirit, through surrendering to God's will.

If we can never surrender to God's will, then we'll never have a free will. A heart that is not single-minded in devotion to God is a bound heart. The freedom to live a healthy life starts by surrendering your will.

This surrendered will is scary only to the degree that we are uncertain of God's love. When we don't trust His love, then we won't trust His will. We will remain slaves. If we trust His love will care for us beyond our ability to care for ourselves, then we'll surrender. When we surrender, we don't lose ourselves—we are finally no longer at war with ourselves. We're free to direct all the things that make us human under the harmony of God's direction.

We are no longer slaves to the lies in our mind, or the things done to us by others. We surrender our right to be self-directed to the guiding hand of God. We train ourselves to embrace a God-given limit. We are no longer the captain of the ship. This gives us a steady capacity to bring the complexities and contradictions of our heart under God's order.

When we surrender to God, His grace flows into us, empowering us to live free. This is a well-kept heart. A well-kept heart allows us to respond in ways that are helpful, and even healing.

We can thrive even when we want to fight back.

We can thrive in moments that require us to choose silence.

We can thrive even when we want to tear someone down.

We can thrive even when someone treats us poorly.

We can thrive even when we're tempted to lie.

We can thrive even when we are tempted to be impatient.

We can thrive even when we're tempted to be resentful.

We can thrive because those who have surrendered their hearts to God know how to find His love in any given situation.

Question

What are some God-given limits in your current season that you might be reluctant to embrace?

_____

Prayer
God, You know me, deeply and thoroughly. You know my wants and my needs. You empower me to lay down my will, knowing that the truest freedom I can find is waiting on the other side of surrender. I ask that You continually show me what it means to live with a well-kept heart. Show me how to maintain it through the power of the Holy Spirit, and not in my own strength. Amen.

Silence
2 minutes of sitting in silence being present to Jesus and yourself.

Presence
Holy Spirit lead me.
Holy Spirit sustain me.
Holy Spirit move through me.

Week Three

Presence

Jesus, still my soul with Your Presence. As You come near, drown out all other voices. Your Presence is enough for me. I will trade all I have for a moment in Your Presence. The worst of life can be endured when I am in Your Presence. The joys of life can be enjoyed when I am in Your Presence. You calm me, and Your Presence is my delight.

Silence

2 minutes of sitting in silence being present to Jesus and yourself.

Worship

Tell Jesus the place He has in your life and what He means to you.

Meditation

Philippians 3:8-9

Read it. Pray it. Ponder it.

Indeed, I count everything as loss because of the surpassing worth of knowing Christ Jesus my Lord. For his sake I have suffered the loss of all things and count them as rubbish, in order that I may gain Christ and be found in him

Scripture: Proverbs 12:

[12] Truthful lips endure forever, but a lying tongue lasts only a moment. (NIV)

Devotional: The Fear of Being Misunderstood

The fear of being misunderstood is so crippling. Sometimes we're afraid of even the potential of being misunderstood.. This threat is powerful enough to keep us self-constrained from the life God tells us we can live.

Here is the flat-out truth: people *will* misunderstand you.

It's going to happen.

If Jesus was misunderstood while being perfect then you and I are definitely going to experience it, too.

I've been a pastor for over 8 years, and every year I hear someone has misunderstood one of my sermons and now has certain assumptions about me. Usually these assumptions aren't good. Even if I know I didn't do anything wrong, people will still have opinions. This is inevitable.

I've realized something as I've tried to overcome this fear. A mature person never uses "I'm just being me" as an excuse to not change something within them–but they're also not a slave to the opinions of people. I will be open to feedback–but being open is different than being enslaved and afraid.

I don't have to live afraid of others' opinions: what's true will stay, and what isn't will fade away. I find comfort in Proverbs 12:19. The truth about me will endure, so wrong opinions have an expiry date and will eventually lose steam.

I cannot control the perceptions of everyone around me. I don't pretend that I am perfect. I will absolutely get things wrong. I will need to grow, and change unhealthy patterns. But that doesn't mean I sit in hiding, trying to polish what others may think of as messy, waiting to make myself perfect before I do anything with my life. I will never be able to guarantee that the crowd will love me, but that's not their job anymore.

I fired them.

I get my love from the Father. He validates me, not them. I must have a deep relationship with God and His affection for me. He will always understand me when the world does not. He gets me when no one else does. My courage is always in proportion to my awareness of God's acceptance.

The bottom line is that God accepts me, and that won't ever change. I don't need a guarantee that the world will accept me. No one ever changed the world by first making sure everyone liked them.

We're not called to preserve our reputation.

We're trying to live the life Jesus asks us to live. This means people will dislike us. I love what my pastor Bill Johnson says, *"If you live by their praises, you'll die by their criticism."*

Let the world misunderstand you while you have a Father who gets you and loves you.

Are you having trouble seeing yourself as accepted and loved by God? Here are some things to reflect upon:

1.) God has forgiven you of everything and holds nothing against you. He isn't punishing you, but He loves you and died for you. How God treated Jesus is exactly how He treats you.

2.) Bring any disqualifying or rejection-based thoughts about yourself to God, and ask Him to speak to you about those areas. Ask Him to show you how He loves you specifically in the areas about yourself you may not love.

3.) The scriptures teach that you are already accepted in Christ—not because you have done life perfectly, but because Christ has—and He has embraced you into His life.

I leave you today with what I tell my son to repeat before he goes to preschool.

I am strong.

I am smart.

I am kind.

I am loved.

Now go and be you.

Question

What does Jesus say about the fear you have about being yourself?

___

Prayer

Jesus, You know me and You love me. You understand me, and I am filled with Your truth. Jesus, take hold of my thoughts– have my full attention. I am led solely by Your opinion of me, and I am guided fully by Your purpose for me. Jesus, I pray that You will continue to come towards me, and may You never stop moving through me. I trust that you will always understand me—and that is more than enough. Amen.

Silence

2 minutes of sitting in silence being present to Jesus and yourself.

Presence

Holy Spirit lead me.
Holy Spirit sustain me.
Holy Spirit move through me.

Week Three
Day 16

Presence

Jesus, still my soul with Your Presence. As You come near, drown out all other voices. Your Presence is enough for me. I will trade all I have for a moment in Your Presence. The worst of life can be endured when I am in Your Presence. The joys of life can be enjoyed when I am in Your Presence. You calm me, and Your Presence is my delight.

Silence

2 minutes of sitting in silence being present to Jesus and yourself.

Worship

Tell Jesus the place He has in your life and what He means to you.

Meditation

Philippians 3:8-9
Read it. Pray it. Ponder it.

Indeed, I count everything as loss because of the surpassing worth of knowing Christ Jesus my Lord. For his sake I have suf-

Matthew 16

fered the loss of all things and count them as rubbish, in order that I may gain Christ and be found in him

Scripture: John 12:1-5

¹ Six days before the Passover, Jesus came to Bethany, where Lazarus lived, whom Jesus raised from the dead. ² Here a dinner was given in Jesus' honor. Martha served, while Lazarus was among those reclining at the table with him. ³ Then Mary took about a pint of pure nard, an expensive perfume; she poured it on Jesus' feet and wiped his feet with her hair. And the house was filled with the fragrance of the perfume. ⁴ But one of his disciples, Judas Iscariot, who was later to betray him, objected, ⁵ "Why wasn't this perfume sold and the money given to the poor? It was worth a year's wages." (NIV)

Devotional: Faith is Offensive

Have you ever been around someone whose passion, extravagant giving, or hope offends you? I remember being in the car with my wife when this happened to me. I can take you to the exact spot where it all went down. We were talking about the car repairs we needed, and we were in a tight financial situation. I wasn't ready to be offended, but her hopeful perspective was about to change me.

"It's all going to be taken care of. Don't worry about it," she said with faith, not optimism.

I am normally a guy who takes risks and believes for the impossible—but not in this exact situation. I unintentionally let

Jesus out of my sight. I tried to be responsible as a husband, but I didn't know I actually picked up fear. I didn't realize it at the moment–but worry feels responsible, and trust feels irresponsible.

She said again, "It's all going to be ok, the money will come in for it."

I was thinking, *"Look at reality!"*

I wanted to look at the facts because they felt like reality. I felt like Peter sinking in the ocean as he considered the waves and took his eyes off Jesus. My faith was only as strong as my answers, and I didn't see a way out. I saw a problem and I was offended by my wife's faith. I was offended because I didn't think she was being real. My wife's answer felt like what you're supposed to say in that situation. I didn't realize she could be looking at Jesus, and speaking to me from faith.

Then God spoke to me.

"Chris, fear is offended by faith."

Once I heard this, I realized I was afraid. I took on too much responsibility, and it clouded me from seeing her faith. I instantly remembered Mary in John 12, who poured perfume on the feet of Jesus. The room was filled with the fragrance of her extravagance– yet one man was offended.

Judas witnessed the passion, extravagance, and faith of Mary firsthand, but kept his offense.

He actually tried to justify his internal frustration by saying she wasted the oil on Jesus, claiming they could have sold it and given to the poor.

Judas was offended and refused to be honest about his offense.

Mary's faith in Jesus hit Judas's false reality with a two-by-four. The faith of others has a way of revealing our issues. The greed and self-preservation within Judas wouldn't allow him to see the beauty of the moment. The invitation of the moment—the invitation Judas missed—was to be intimate with Jesus instead of merely being near Him.

There's a difference between being in proximity to Jesus and being intimate with Jesus. In proximity, we're close enough to see what's going on, but our dignity keeps us from opening our hearts. Intimacy is when you do and think what seems unreasonable because you trust Him.

My wife had faith, and I had fear.

I was frustrated that she had the right response to the situation. She was intimate with Jesus, knowing that He would care for us. I was frustrated she had that kind of trust. My heart needed humbling to recognize the invitation from my wife's faith. I was being invited into faith, but I had to recognize her own first. Intimacy with God requires we keep an open heart and celebrate the passion, extravagance, and faith of others.

We must let go of worry as responsibility, and be inspired—not offended—by the faith of others.

How can you be inspired by someone around you whose passion, extravagant giving, or hope offends you?

Prayer

Jesus, I am continually made new by your ways. Though I sometimes find myself offended, your redemptive love leads me back to my seat at your side. Jesus, I repent for choosing facts above faith and I release fear from my heart. Jesus, I submit myself to your will and I lean into trusting you fully. Jesus, just as Mary poured perfume on your feet, I pour my life at yours. I am coming into complete vulnerability with you, and I choose to stay there. Amen.

Silence

2 minutes of sitting in silence being present to Jesus and yourself.

Presence

Holy Spirit lead me.
Holy Spirit sustain me.
Holy Spirit move through me.

Week Three

Day 17

Presence

Jesus, still my soul with Your Presence. As You come near, drown out all other voices. Your Presence is enough for me. I will trade all I have for a moment in Your Presence. The worst of life can be endured when I am in Your Presence. The joys of life can be enjoyed when I am in Your Presence. You calm me, and Your Presence is my delight.

Silence

2 minutes of sitting in silence being present to Jesus and yourself.

Worship

Tell Jesus the place He has in your life and what He means to you.

Meditation

Philippians 3:8-9

Read it. Pray it. Ponder it.

Indeed, I count everything as loss because of the surpassing worth of knowing Christ Jesus my Lord. For his sake I have suffered the loss of all things and count them as rubbish, in order that I may gain Christ and be found in him

Scripture: James 2:14-18

¹⁴ What good is it, my brothers, if someone says he has faith but does not have works? Can that faith save him? ¹⁵ If a brother or sister is poorly clothed and lacking in daily food, 16 and one of you says to them, "Go in peace, be warmed and filled," without giving them the things needed for the body, what good is that? ¹⁷ So also faith by itself, if it does not have works, is dead.

18 But someone will say, "You have faith and I have works." Show me your faith apart from your works, and I will show you my faith by my work. (ESV)

Devotional: Comfort and Obedience

How we respond to God's invitations in life matters. Whenever we resist God, we actually comfort our fears. In fact, our comfort zone is usually the reason we resist being obedient to God.

Saul of Tarsus–who was capturing and overseeing the stoning of Christians–regained his sight only because Ananias followed God's direction into the unknown. Ananias had to sacrifice what was comfortable and safe. And, in case you're wondering, God is still doing this to His disciples today. He invites us into situations *where He can make a difference through us*–knowing it could cost us.

One time I was at a burrito joint, with barely enough money for my own meal. As I arrived to the register, God said to me, "Pay for the man behind you." I could tell this man was struggling, but I had very little money to give away. I knew God was already aware of my own limitations–and He invited me to be generous anyway.

In those few seconds, I was processing the fear of not having enough money. I was juggling this guy's needs in one hand, and my own financial security in the other. The invitation to make a difference was right there, but my fear stood in the way.

I began asking myself if it was really God speaking to me. We often do that when we're afraid. We wonder if God is talking to us, or if we're just making it up. It's easier to justify denying yourself than it is to acknowledge you're ignoring God.

If we believe our thoughts are flesh-initiated, and not God-initiated, we can pretend our negligence is faithfulness. It's a lot easier to comfort fear by claiming we're not hearing God.

I finally decided to pay for the man's meal and simply told him, "This is just to let you know that there are still good people in the world."

Walking back, I chatted with God. During the conversation, I realized fear is uncertainty in the nature of God. It's our Father's good pleasure to take care of His children. I was afraid to give that guy money because I wasn't confident that God would take care of me. When we lack confidence in who God is, we lack the courage to overcome fear. The courage to follow God's invitation, and to trust in His nature, will always feel like a sacrifice at first.

The Apostle Paul actually tells the Corinthian church, "For we who live are constantly being delivered over to death for Jesus' sake, so that the life of Jesus also may be manifested in our mortal flesh. So death works in us, but life in you" (2 Corinthians 4:10-12 NASB). He's telling them there are parts of Christ that will never be formed in us unless we are willing to sacrifice.

Jesus is manifested in us through our sacrifice.

Those who are willing to pay a price will be the ones who pave a road. All our sacrifices will be different—we are rarely called to sacrifice the same thing as someone else. God knows what kind of sacrifice will best express the fragrance of Christ in our example–so it would be wrong to reduce one kind of invitation to a universal principle that everyone has to adhere to. I simply know this: *sacrifice is a non-negotiable for having Christ formed in you.*

What's one step you can take today to get out of your comfort zone?

Prayer

Jesus, I trust that You are good–even when things feel out of my control, and out of my comfort zone. The guiding truth that You are good will never change, because You never change. My obedience and surrender to You is my honor, not my disadvantage. And when I am holding onto this world too tightly, let Your Spirit remind me what is eternally significant. I ask that you push me out of my fears, and use me to make a difference in others. Amen.

Silence

2 minutes of sitting in silence being present to Jesus and yourself.

Presence

Holy Spirit lead me.
Holy Spirit sustain me.
Holy Spirit move through me.

Week Three

Day 18

Presence

Jesus, still my soul with Your Presence. As You come near, drown out all other voices. Your Presence is enough for me. I will trade all I have for a moment in Your Presence. The worst of life can be endured when I am in Your Presence. The joys of life can be enjoyed when I am in Your Presence. You calm me, and Your Presence is my delight.

Silence

2 minutes of sitting in silence being present to Jesus and yourself.

Worship

Tell Jesus the place He has in your life and what He means to you.

Philippians 3:8-9

Read it. Pray it. Ponder it.

Indeed, I count everything as loss because of the surpassing worth of knowing Christ Jesus my Lord. For his sake I have suffered the loss of all things and count them as rubbish, in order that I may gain Christ and be found in him

Scripture: Mark 5:25-34

[25] And there was a woman who had had a discharge of blood for twelve years, [26] and who had suffered much under many physicians, and had spent all that she had, and was no better but rather grew worse. [27] She had heard the reports about Jesus and came up behind him in the crowd and touched his garment. [28] For she said, "If I touch even his garments, I will be made well." [29] And immediately the flow of blood dried up, and she felt in her body that she was healed of her disease. [30] And Jesus, perceiving in himself that power had gone out from him, immediately turned about in the crowd and said, "Who touched my garments?" [31] And his disciples said to him, "You see the crowd pressing around you, and yet you say, 'Who touched me?'" [32] And he looked

around to see who had done it. [33] But the woman, knowing what had happened to her, came in fear and trembling and fell down before him and told him the whole truth. [34] And he said to her, "Daughter, your faith has made you well; go in peace, and be healed of your disease." (ESV)

Devotional: Discerning the Holy Spirit

Have you ever felt like God isn't moving?

Me too.

The question isn't whether or not God is moving. The question is: are we paying attention?

Sometimes, the ordinary stillness we overlook is actually the precipice of our next encounter. He actually sets up these moments to invite us to engage. These sorts of opportunities have been some of the greatest times in my life: I've seen God heal deaf ears on the side of the road because we recognized that sharing the same stoplight was our divine appointment. I've ended up baptizing young men under waterfalls in Puerto Rico and in the swimming lanes at our local YMCA. God does not always announce these moments with trumpets and angels. Most of the miraculous moments I've experienced began in ordinary, simple ways.

It feels so good to seize these kinds of moments–but they can be confusing. The Holy Spirit is teaching us how to discern when we are being drawn to the edge of the miraculous.

My life moves fast–sometimes too fast–and the priority of remaining present to the Spirit is often difficult. Here's why: God will not force us to notice these kinds of moments. I love the story of Jesus walking through a crowd, when a woman reaches out to touch Him for her miracle.

Jesus asks, "Who touched me?"

His disciples are like, "Are you kidding me?"

But Jesus was aware of something they weren't. The Bible describes it as "power [going] out from Him". Everyone was touching Him, but one person *touched* Him. Jesus had to be so aware of Himself and the Holy Spirit to be able to recognize a God-touch above everyone else's touch. He was so present to God's Spirit that He knew to stop–because something significant had taken place within Him.

Seizing divine moments starts with us remaining present to the Holy Spirit.

We are capable of stopping, just like Jesus did, when we know something is changing within ourselves–and we can discern God's Spirit. Discernment can be like an unused muscle for some, and it can feel overwhelming to start. But you're designed to use it. As an athlete, I needed to develop muscle memory. I needed to be so in tune with the moment that I could act before even thinking.

Discernment is not a religious rule, like, "Think about God, think about God, think about God!" It's a conscious choice to say, *"God, I want to discern you and whatever you have for me."*

Since beginning this practice, I have had some incredible God moments that have changed me forever. I've watched someone I just met pull their drugs out of their pocket and throw them over a bridge–choosing to follow Jesus out of their addiction–because I merely said yes to the Holy Spirit's prompting. This all starts with developing a sensitivity to the Spirit.

We need to learn what it means to simply discern Him.

It can begin by slowing down your day. Ask yourself to look for something you never noticed before. This sort of observation will help exercise that muscle. Awareness gets us out of the autopilot of life that misses the Spirit's invitation into the miraculous.

Pay attention to how your body feels when you worship–God moments can feel very similar to how you feel in that setting. The atmosphere of worship trains our sensitivity to His presence. This isn't about enthroning a sensation, but discerning how your body reacts to God's Spirit. Jesus knew something had gone out from Him.

Remember: Jesus wasn't on His way to heal her. The Bible teaches us that Jesus only did what He saw the Father doing. We sometimes imagine Jesus received a daily checklist from God that gave Him a plan without any detours or surprises.

Instead, Jesus spent time with the Father, and knew what the Father's work felt like. When Jesus was walking past this woman, He discerned what felt like the Father's work. He cooperated with it, and did what the Father was doing. This interaction was not initiated by Jesus–but it was discerned by Him.

It's time to take a risk. You will always wonder what sort of moments you are missing until you try, and sometimes we get it wrong. But getting it wrong is okay. Try, and try again. Start building a personal history with God. Risk the possibility that you are beginning to hear Him over the fear that you aren't. Follow the impressions you get in the ordinary moments of life, and over time, you will learn what is and what isn't from God.

Question

What is one way that you discern the Holy Spirit in your day?

Prayer

Jesus, I am found in Your presence. You steady my heart and you calm my mind. Jesus, You settle my busyness and stand above my ambitions. I am listening for Your direction, and I am committed to Your instruction. Jesus, I hear you in the stillness–and I reach out to grab You in the chaos. I will follow You, Holy Spirit. I want to do what You're doing, Jesus. I ask for Your help to discern Your Presence throughout my day. Amen.

Silence

2 minutes of sitting in silence being present to Jesus and yourself.

Presence

Holy Spirit lead me.
Holy Spirit sustain me.
Holy Spirit move through me.

Presence

Jesus, still my soul with Your Presence. As You come near, drown out all other voices. Your Presence is enough for me. I will trade all I have for a moment in Your Presence. The worst of life can be endured when I am in Your Presence. The joys of life can be enjoyed when I am in Your Presence. You calm me, and Your Presence is my delight.

Silence

2 minutes of sitting in silence being present to Jesus and yourself.

Worship

Tell Jesus the place He has in your life and what He means to you.

Meditation

Philippians 3:8-9

Read it. Pray it. Ponder it.

Indeed, I count everything as loss because of the surpassing worth of knowing Christ Jesus my Lord. For his sake I have suffered the loss of all things and count them as rubbish, in order that I may gain Christ and be found in him

Scripture: Acts 9:13-16

[13] But Ananias answered, "Lord, I have heard from many about this man, how much evil he has done to your saints at

Jerusalem. [14] And here he has authority from the chief priests to bind all who call on your name." [15] But the Lord said to him, "Go, for he is a chosen instrument of mine to carry my name before the Gentiles and kings and the children of Israel. [16] For I will show him how much he must suffer for the sake of my name." (ESV)

Devotional: Living in a Bubble

Have you ever seen the movie Bubble Boy? The one with Jake Gyllenhaal–not the one with the full-haired John Travolta.

It's probably not worth watching. But it presents a perfect introduction for what we're going to consider together.

(This is your friendly spoiler alert.)

The story is about a boy who is born without immunities. To protect him from getting sick, he has spent all of his life in a plastic bubble. He's made fun of by other kids, he lacks a real social life, and he never leaves his home. Then, in the most predictable way, he falls in love. The only problem: the girl he loves is getting married to the wrong guy! (Yes, it's one of those movies.) His love for her sends him on a mission to break up the wedding.

He goes on a crazy journey, and eventually gets to the wedding. Upon arrival, he gets out of his mobile bubble suit, kisses the girl of his dreams and immediately passes out. Everyone assumes he's dead, because of his lack of immunities. But when our hero wakes up in the hospital, his mother confesses that his immune system developed by the age of four. She lied to him to keep him safe. She didn't want him to be "corrupted" by the world.

The boy's bubble suit curbed the fears of his family–but it also imprisoned him. The boy, in turn, welcomed the limitations given to him. He watched the world pass him by in the safety of his bubble, although the safety it provided him was a fiction. The world has it's problems, sure. But when we see someone living in a bubble, we all want to shout, *"Get out!"*

At the end of the movie, when he finally gets out, the boy says, *"I'd rather spend one minute holding you than the rest of my life knowing I never could."*

Life is not lived in bubbles.

The only way to experience the world is to open ourselves up to risk. Our comfort zones make for safe days, but missed adventures. Bubbles keep the world from marking us–but they also prevent us from leaving our mark upon the world. You have to step outside of your comfort zone to make the difference you're designed to make. You have to take off the bubble suit and kiss the girl, man! Well, metaphorically speaking.

The truth is this: no one has ever changed the world through easy choices.

Breaking our addiction to safe decisions is the biggest hurdle to being a catalyst for the Kingdom of God. We have to break free from the need for guarantees. It's not that you don't need security in life–but your desire for security can't always sit in the driver's seat. God doesn't invite us into a safe, predictable, and easy life.

In Acts 9, a certain disciple named Ananias is asked by God to pray for a violent persecutor of the church named Saul.

This is a crazy request! Upon hearing this, Ananias is concerned for his own life. Saul is killing Christians, but God hasn't given up on Saul.

God's heart for Saul needed the courage of a willing person. He invited Ananias into this moment. God was pressing on the seams of Ananias's bubble. Guarantees were placed on the altar. It's as if God took Ananias to a cliff and said, "Jump." God wanted Ananias's loyalty before he could guarantee Ananias's success.

The rest of the story is history. Ananias ministers to this once violent man, and he helps send Saul on a new course. Saul will change his name to Paul, and get his own wild ride of changing the world. This one moment—where Ananaias stepped out of his small bubble and trusted God with his safety—ended up changing the course of history.

We have to confront our comforts. God isn't a killjoy, but we can be trapped in our safe and predictable lives. Obedience only feels hard when we think we can run our lives better than Jesus. God is eager to see you break out of your bubble.

Question

What are the bubbles you have created in your life that keep you "safe", but out of the adventure of faith?

Prayer

Jesus, I was made to live by faith. I will stand in the tension, and proclaim Your name over my doubts. Fear is not my master—Jesus, You are. I am made to proactively bring heaven to earth—and that is not done in comfort. Jesus, I lean into the unexpected, expecting to encounter You. Jesus, I am chosen by You–and I celebrate the victories we will have. I am so thankful to be in union with You, Jesus. Amen.

Silence
2 minutes of sitting in silence being present to Jesus and yourself.

Presence
Holy Spirit lead me.
Holy Spirit sustain me.
Holy Spirit move through me.

Week Three
Day 20

Presence
Jesus, still my soul with Your Presence. As You come near, drown out all other voices. Your Presence is enough for me. I will trade all I have for a moment in Your Presence. The worst of life can be endured when I am in Your Presence. The joys of life can be enjoyed when I am in Your Presence. You calm me, and Your Presence is my delight.

Silence
2 minutes of sitting in silence being present to Jesus and yourself.

Worship
Tell Jesus the place He has in your life and what He means to you.

Meditation

Philippians 3:8-9

Read it. Pray it. Ponder it.

Indeed, I count everything as

Psalm of the week **84**

loss because of the surpassing worth of knowing Christ Jesus my Lord. For his sake I have suffered the loss of all things and count them as rubbish, in order that I may gain Christ and be found in him

Scripture: 2 Corinthians 1:3-4

[3] Praise be to the God and Father of our Lord Jesus Christ, the Father of compassion and the God of all comfort, [4] who comforts us in all our troubles, so that we can comfort those in any trouble with the comfort we ourselves receive from God. (NIV)

Devotional: Part of the Solution

Jesus doesn't heal you just for you.

Jesus doesn't transform you just for you.

He wants to heal the world—so, He first healed you.

Jesus has a trajectory for every human within His plan to renew all things. His trajectory includes converting us from being someone who only receives into someone who gives. He doesn't just make the thief stop stealing—He transforms the thief into a contributor who lives to benefit the good of all.

What Jesus has done in us should eventually flow through us. He wants the world to know Him and His love through us. He wants to become visible. The paradoxical thing is that Jesus isn't invisible. The Scriptures tell us He has a body. He is healing this body so we can display Him well.

Jesus isn't in a rush with what He is doing inside of us. The renovation within takes time, but God never abandons the idea of moving through us. God has no problem with our learning process, but He does have a problem with passivity.

God can do anything in this world without us, but He has humbly invited us to join His work. That means you and I are part of the solution. God rarely thinks of solutions absent of people. He doesn't see us as a distraction to His will. He wants us to participate in it.

God prefers to demonstrate Himself to your world through you.

Moses is a great example. When God told Moses about His plan to deliver Israel, He said *"I have come to rescue them... So, now go. I am sending you."* Moses is integral to God's plan for Israel's freedom.

God is thinking about you when He is thinking of helping others.

We can pray that Jesus brings a person comfort without seeing how He wants us to bring the comfort. The Holy Spirit does something unique inside of us: He converts us into a dispenser of His breakthrough. The work Jesus does in our personal lives should eventually translate into the ministry we give to others– because as my pastor Bill Johnson says, *"You're a river, not a lake."*

The Apostle Paul describes this reality by declaring that the *"God of all comfort...comforts us in all our troubles so that we can comfort those in any trouble with the comfort we ourselves receive from God."*

If you notice, Paul doesn't say "God comforts all of us." It's important we understand that God wants to get His comfort to all who are broken. But He is not insecure. He shares the load. We're comforted not so that we can just pray that others are comforted. We're meant to take that comfort and release it to others who need God's comfort.

Here is the punchline of it all: God will not bypass what He has decided to do through you.

People around you need you to convert from only receiving comfort, to becoming a generous dispenser of God's comfort–by bringing Heaven to earth.

Question

What is something you've received from God that you can release to others?

Prayer

God, You know me and You love me well. For I am loved for my sake, but I am anointed for the world's sake. I will make Your name known. God, I am present to the pain of this world, and I recognize that I carry part of the solution. I join in on Your redemptive plan. God, I follow your signs and I trust in Your leading. I ask that You would show me how I can make a difference. I exist to bring Heaven to Earth and I long to learn how to do it. Jesus, be my teacher and guide to bring comfort to the broken. Amen.

Silence

2 minutes of sitting in silence being present to Jesus and yourself.

Presence

Holy Spirit lead me.
Holy Spirit sustain me.
Holy Spirit move through me.

Week Three

Day 21

Presence

Jesus, still my soul with Your Presence. As You come near, drown out all other voices. Your Presence is enough for me. I will trade all I have for a moment in Your Presence. The worst of life can be endured when I am in Your Presence. The joys of life can be enjoyed when I am in Your Presence. You calm me, and Your Presence is my delight.

Silence

2 minutes of sitting in silence being present to Jesus and yourself.

Worship

Tell Jesus the place He has in your life and what He means to you.

Meditation

Philippians 3:8-9

Read it. Pray it. Ponder it.

Indeed, I count everything as loss because of the surpassing worth of knowing Christ Jesus my Lord. For his sake I have suffered the loss of all things and count them as rubbish, in order that I may gain Christ and be found in him

Scripture: 1 Corinthians 13:1-8

1 If I speak in the tongues of men or of angels, but do not have love, I am only a resounding gong or a clanging cymbal. 2 If I have the gift of prophecy and can fathom all mysteries and all knowledge, and if I have a faith that can move mountains, but do not have love, I am nothing. 3 If I give all I possess to the poor and give over my body to hardship that I may boast, but do not have love, I gain nothing.

4 Love is patient, love is kind. It does not envy, it does not boast, it is not proud. 5 It does not dishonor others, it is not self-seeking, it is not easily angered, it keeps no record of wrongs. 6 Love does not delight in evil but rejoices with the truth. 7 It always protects, always trusts, always hopes, always perseveres.

8 Love never fails. (NIV)

Devotional: Love One Another

When you begin to spend time with Jesus, you quickly discover He loves people well. You learn He doesn't get hung up on how much it will cost Him, or what people will do with His love. He loves freely because that's who He is. Saint Ignatius said, *"God is love loving."* This such a great way of understanding God's love.

He is actively loving you. He is actively speaking words of care, affection, and strength to you.

He is actively doing what will make the best outcome for you. He is actively giving Himself for you, to know how valuable you are to Him.

Jesus doesn't hoard His love.

He shares it.

Jesus loves so extravagantly it costs Him His life. He doesn't love within what's comfortable. He doesn't preserve Himself from the cost of love. His love is not calculated, and His love is not burdensome.

Jesus didn't ask how little love could He get away with before He felt uncomfortable. He opened His heart to those who might never love Him back, because He wasn't loving to get something in return. He was loving them for them. Thomas Merton said, *"Love seeks one thing: the good of the one loved. Love is not a feeling or desire, it's to will the good of others."*

This can honestly be frightening because we're still learning to be possessed by love. And to whatever degree that we're not surrendering to love, we will not truly be loving of others. Jesus wants to reform our entire being so that love isn't simply something that we do, but the grace which animates our entire life. As we pursue love, we become kind, patient, and forgiving. We become willing to do whatever increases the wellbeing of the subject of our affection. If their wellbeing needs patience, then our pursuit of love energizes us to be patient.

Jesus invites us into a new way of being in the world. We can be in the world in all sorts of ways. We can be fearful. We can be angry. We can be selfish. He wants us to be loving. Jesus said, *"A new command I give you: Love one another. As I have loved you, so you must love one another."*

God's love starts to take ahold of us, and we begin to overcome all our self-protection. We begin to overcome all our fears about love, and what it might cost us. We move beyond the idea that love is a feeling. As Dallas Willard said, *"I do not come to my enemy and then try to love them, I come to them as a loving person."*

A person who is loving isn't self-preserving. A loving person is ready to endure and bear hardships as they love. Because love is selfless, love is not painless. It will cost us—but love is the only thing worth that kind of cost. If we were to give up on love—instead of leaning into the cost of love—we would be asking God to give up on us.

We must, as the Apostle Paul said, *"Pursue love."*

Question

What self-protecting and self-preserving lies do you have about loving others?

Prayer

Jesus, I exist to love the way You loved. As You loved the woman at the well. As You loved the soldiers who arrested you. As You loved the world by giving up Your life. Help me to overcome my self-protecting thoughts about loving people. I desire to be a person of deep love. Jesus, teach me be vulnerable enough to love people without reserve. I want to approach the world with open arms. I am so thankful for the way You have loved me. Amen.

Silence

2 minutes of sitting in silence being present to Jesus and yourself.

Presence

Holy Spirit lead me.
Holy Spirit sustain me.
Holy Spirit move through me.

Week
Four

Presence

Jesus, hold me. I desire to be comforted by Your Presence. When I am in Your arms, I know I am well. You satisfy me. You alone carry words of life. I cannot go on without You. My whole being thirsts to drink from Your living water. Jesus, Your embrace heals me. You're the Shepherd of my soul.

Silence

2 minutes of sitting in silence being present to Jesus and yourself.

Worship

Tell Jesus the place He has in your life and what He means to you.

Meditation

Isaiah 43: 1-2

Read it. Pray it. Ponder it.

I have called you by your name; You are Mine. When you pass through the waters, I will be with you; And through the rivers, they shall not overflow you. When you walk through the fire, you shall not be burned, Nor shall the flame scorch you.

Scripture: Acts 10:38

[38] God anointed Jesus of Nazareth with the Holy Spirit and power, and he went around doing good and healing all who were under the power of the devil, because God was with him. (NIV)

Devotional: Destroying The Works of The Devil

Jesus has a paradigm that is often lost in our modern culture. He understood the reality of the devil.

This is important.

Jon Tyson says, *"If you don't have room for the devil in your understanding of the gospel you will end up making people the enemy."*

Jesus didn't overplay the devil, but He didn't neglect Him either.

Jesus did what He saw the Father doing–He was not just reacting to what He saw the devil doing. Jesus is Spirit-led, not devil-led. This means He didn't go around blaming the devil for everything or talking about how much the devil was out to get Him.

Jesus talked about the devil whenever He was confronting the demonic reality at hand. Jesus is anointed to destroy darkness. He revealed that the Kingdom of God is willing to confront the kingdom of darkness.

Jesus made God's Kingdom known by demonstrating it. Jesus pursued impossible situations.

He displayed this by destroying the works of the devil through the power of the Holy Spirit. Jesus showed humans that they were meant to join in on God's unfolding plan of renewing all things and confronting the powers that try to sway them off-course. When Jesus released the Spirit, He in turn displaced the darkness. We cannot ignore the great lengths to which the Gospels go to reveal this spiritual conflict to us. We read of exorcisms, healings, and miracles of various kinds. Jesus was no stranger to the impossible.

In fact, He found a home in the impossible.

The Apostle Paul teaches that part of our faith in God must be rooted in demonstrations of His Spirit and power. We need to remove our over-dependency on our natural abilities. This means we don't just depend on God when we face an impossible situation–we pursue impossible situations, trusting in the power of God to come through for us.

Jesus lived a normal life with God. He recognized the devil's work was present on earth and it needed to be destroyed. In our lack of experience in the power of the Spirit, we've become overdependent on our own efforts, and overly accommodating to darkness.

Jesus would heal the sick, instead of offering a theological rationale for the sickness.

Jesus would raise the dead, instead of debating whether such a miracle was feasible or not.

Jesus would cast out demons, instead of handing out self-help books to help people make peace with their internal torment.

The incredible Evangelist Reinhard Bonnke was once in a room of theologians, and they asked for his theological position on a certain debate in the Church. Bonnke's response shakes my insides. He said, *"I will split hairs in heaven when I am done breaking chains on earth."* We can't tolerate the work of the devil. There can be no accommodation for it, nor any compromise, in the life of a disciple of Jesus. We're not impressed with it. We're commissioned to destroy it.

If we spend any amount of time with Jesus we will soon run into Him talking about the power given to us to defeat the darkness plaguing the lives of those we love. We will soon recognize that He talks with authority because He doesn't tolerate darkness like we do.

This is the normal Christian life as Jesus revealed it. We're not at a disadvantage. Sometimes, I don't think the devil is our real threat. Our tolerance for his remnant of influence is our real threat. Our over-satisfaction with good theology is our real threat. Our compulsion to make Church all about us and our family is our real threat. The lengths to which we go to make Sunday merely a fun experience is our real threat. Our desire for seats to be filled over power displayed is our real threat. Our fear of what people will think is our real threat.

The devil knows he has lost. He wants to convince you he hasn't.

Question

Where has God called you to destroy the works of the enemy?

Prayer

Jesus, I trust that through Your power in me, I no longer have to fear impossible situations. Just like You made a home in the impossible, teach me how to walk in the power of the Holy Spirit. Give me eyes to see, ears to hear, hands to heal, and a mouth to speak the mysteries of Heaven. Jesus, show me how possible it is to break chains on earth. Amen.

Silence

2 minutes of sitting in silence being present to Jesus and yourself.

Presence

Holy Spirit lead me.
Holy Spirit sustain me.
Holy Spirit move through me.

Week Four

Day 23

Presence

Jesus, hold me. I desire to be comforted by Your Presence. When I am in Your arms, I know I am well. You satisfy me. You alone carry words of life. I cannot go on without You. My whole being thirsts to drink from Your living water. Jesus, Your embrace heals me. You're the Shepherd of my soul.

Silence

2 minutes of sitting in silence being present to Jesus and yourself.

Worship

Tell Jesus the place He has in your life and what He means to you.

Psalm of the week **103**

Matthew **23**

Meditation

Isaiah 43: 1-2
Read it. Pray it. Ponder it.

I have called you by your name; You are Mine. When you pass through the waters, I will be with you; And through the rivers, they shall not overflow you. When

**you walk through the fire, you
shall not be burned, Nor shall
the flame scorch you.**

Scripture: Matthew 8:23-24

[23] And when he got into the boat, his disciples followed him. [24] And behold, there arose a great storm on the sea, so that the boat was being swamped by the waves; but he was asleep. (NASB)

Devotional: Peace in The Storm

In the midst of chaos, we often find ourselves grappling for peace. Our souls ache to settle and rest during the storms of our lives. The truth is, we will always have cares, worries, and circumstances that are beyond our control. Is peace even possible? If so, where do we find it?

I was on a train in New York City when God spoke to me. At the time I was experiencing pain because someone I knew was going through something completely out of my control. I wanted to fix it. I had a mountain I wanted to be moved, a valley I needed to be filled. I was feeling the weight of this problem and I was anxious for relief.

In my anxiety, I began to come up with solutions that I thought could change it. I wanted to fix what was outside of my control with what was in my control in order to have peace. Right in the middle of this, God said, *"You don't realize I care about this more than you do. You're trying to gain peace by your own efforts because you don't trust Me."*

Those words felt like a spear piercing my heart. I was under the illusion of a few lies. One being that I cared more about this situation than God did, and the other being that peace would only come once change happened.

I didn't realize how I lost sight of God's commitment to me. I didn't have peace because I didn't trust He was watching me. I had been trusting in my own abilities to give my heart rest. Like the woman at the well, I was focused on my immediate, human needs–neglecting Jesus's offer for the living water that would quench my soul's thirst for peace. He knew it was more than possible for me to have the peace that I craved.

I forgot that my peace only lasts when it comes through Him. In that moment of stark realization, I knew I had to lay down all my efforts, tactics, and strategies to "get" the peace I wanted. I had to *"cast my cares upon Him because He cares for me."*

I had an internal longing for what God wanted to give me, but my mistrust drove me to my own devices. We are always left wanting more when we don't trust God.

We must realize that Jesus is the only drink that makes all other wells go dry. He satisfies in ways we never could experience on our own. Jesus enjoys the same peace He offers to us. This is how Jesus could sleep in the middle of a storm.

Question

What problem do you think you care about more than God does?

___

Prayer
God, You have countless ways to calm my storms, and I rest in this truth. I marvel at Your wondrous ways, and I am

thankful for Your unending grace. I receive the freedom You have for me, and I surrender my control. God, my peace is your responsibility—and I rest in knowing you are not far from me or my needs. You guard my peace, You guard my joy, and You guard my thanksgiving. God, You have made me rich in patience and I am well-fed in hope. I am thankful for Your unconditional pursuit. God, You are all I need in the storm. Amen.

Silence

2 minutes of sitting in silence being present to Jesus and yourself.

Presence

Holy Spirit lead me.
Holy Spirit sustain me.
Holy Spirit move through me.

Week Four

Day 24

Presence

Jesus, hold me. I desire to be comforted by Your Presence. When I am in Your arms, I know I am well. You satisfy me. You alone carry words of life. I cannot go on without You. My whole being thirsts to drink from Your living water. Jesus, Your embrace heals me. You're the Shepherd of my soul.

Silence

2 minutes of sitting in silence being present to Jesus and yourself.

Worship

Tell Jesus the place He has in your life and what He means to you.

I have called you by your name; You are Mine. When you pass through the waters, I will be with you; And through the rivers, they shall not overflow you. When you walk through the fire, you shall not be burned, Nor shall the flame scorch you.

Scripture: John 14:9

[9] Jesus said to him, "Have I been with you for so long, and you still do not know me, Philip? Whoever has seen me has seen the Father." (ESV)

Devotional: The Revelation of God in Christ

On a random and uneventful evening, Heaven was eager.

The Holy Spirit rushed into my life and took me straight into the heart of God.

Death and resurrection were my portions that night.

I was a new person.

The Holy Spirit buried an unsatisfied, wounded life, and raised me into an otherworldly kind of existence.

I began walking on a new road that night–a road paved with a passion for knowing God.

I was a college student at the time. I thought good grades, success, money, or any other blessings were determined by whether or not God was pleased with me. The lack of those things in my life was a sign of His disappointment. Plainly put, my shortcomings led me to fear His vengeance. He was forgiving, but He was also punishing. I loved God, but I was still afraid of Him.

Have you ever been there?

I craved clarity—my heart needed a resolve. I felt in over my head. I needed my image of God to undergo a radical re-vision. My theology was anchored to altar calls from fran-tic pastors calling me to appease God's vengeance. I didn't know anything else.

My unsettled heart manifested in my worship. I treated my time with God as a confession booth. It's how I kept Him at bay. I anticipated His vengeance before His mercy. I as-sumed His blessings were delayed, or postponed until further notice. Trusting Him made me weary, because my sin turned Him into Zeus. He threw bolts of lightning from the heavens in the form of bad grades and unfortunate setbacks. In my heart of hearts, I knew this picture of God needed to change. I couldn't survive the mood swings of heaven.

My soul was asking what the great theologian A.W. Tozer said is the *"gravest question before [man]...what he in his deep heart conceives God to be like."* I didn't expect what God would uncover for me. I had no clue how God wanted to reveal Himself.

This radical revision of God's image began when I heard Bill Johnson say, *"Jesus is perfect theology."*

This tore through my traditional thoughts on God and the Cross. I felt shoved by the Holy Spirit to reconsider the Scriptures and the assumptions of my theology. I felt urged to go past my former perceptions, and I found what felt like an entirely different God.

God wanted to save me from "God"–the false idol I made of Him.

I learned a radical truth, offensive to all religions of the world: Jesus is God's self-revelation. God is best known in Jesus. God, revealed in His heart of hearts, is exactly like Jesus. This truth changes everything. It tells me Jesus isn't the nice side of God, but the full definition of God's self-expression. I started devouring the Gospels, the New Testament's weighty descriptions of grace, and Jesus Himself as the image of the invisible God.

I found out Jesus isn't the sideshow of heaven. He isn't trying to distract us from His vengeful Father, and He isn't the "good cop" who makes criminals feel safe. He's the exact imprint of God's divine nature! Jesus's life and ministry–culminating in the Crucifixion– unravelled the flawed and deceptive interpretations of God's character. I would dare say the self-sacrificing love shown in the crucifixion is what God had in mind as our theological cornerstone.

Christ frames the entire conversation on the nature of God. The Father intended us to be confident in His nature by what we see in Christ. The reality of the incarnation of the Word of God rearranged every thought I've ever had about Him. I finally met the Father revealed in the light of the Son, and the scales fell from my eyes as my deception faded away.

Jesus enlightens us to the Father's true nature.

We can see with new eyes. He's loving–full of mercy and grace. God desires to be known not by his anger, but by His self-sacrificing love. Known for taking our sin upon Himself rather than punishing us for it.

Two events in the gospel narrative really helped fuel the overcoming of my deception of a vengeful God.

The first is in the gospel of John chapter 8: the woman caught in the act of adultery.

The woman is caught in sin, and the religious leaders think God's plan for her is death. They want to inflict vengeance on God's behalf by throwing stones at her. It was how they saw God, and it seemed a lot like the God I knew in college. These Pharisees, who thought they understood God's character, brought her before Jesus.

Jesus, the self-revelation of the Father, gives the entire audience permission to kill the woman–under one criterion. The man without sin can throw the first stone. Jesus says they can follow through with their judgment, and execute her. But only the one who can stand under that criteria can render the verdict. That person alone has the right to judge her.

I don't know if you caught it: Jesus was talking about Himself. He was the only one without sin. He had the right to punish her–and if He did, then He would have confirmed God's vengeance toward us. But Jesus didn't stone her. Those ready to condemn her left, one by one. He picked her up and pointed out that her condemners had left. The only one left–who had the right to stone her–forgave her.

This is crazy. Before, if I even looked at a woman wrong, I anticipated a week of chaos. Seeing Jesus like this shook me up. My image of God before Christ was ready to throw stones. Heck, I even thought Jesus would be willing to throw a few. Jesus enlightened the Father's nature to me–and He pressed the delete button on my vengeful image of God.

The next event that changed my perception was the Crucifixion narrative, and the last words of Jesus before death.

In Luke 23:34, Jesus said, *"Father, forgive them, for they do not know what they are doing."*

A murdered God's famous last words.

Those are the words Jesus labored to utter at His moment of death, at the hands of bloodthirsty, violent Romans. An innocent man, mudered on the cross. Vengeance feels like a proportionate response to me–but it wasn't for Jesus.

He was handed every right, by the standard of fair justice, to give an equal retribution. If there was a moment to start an insurrection and burn the city out of righteous vengeance, this was it. It was man's worst crime: the killing of God! Sinners had their way with Christ. They knew He was innocent, and they could find no fault in Him–and yet they killed Love anyway.

Jesus's nature, in response to their nature, brings the true God into focus. When we see Jesus on the Cross as the fullest picture of what God is like, His words land with such a convicting blow that they eradicate any remaining fear of His vengeance. Jesus' last words fall upon His oppressors, telling them there's a way back–whether or not they decide to take it. His justice wasn't an eye for an eye. He left them with no concern for His revenge.

But He left them with a way out, telling them He didn't count this against them.

This kind of violence and murder creates tyrants out of men—but for God, it became the ultimate showcase of His character. God decided He wanted His reconciling love to be the signature of His nature. I love how Miroslav Volf, a Croatian theologian and Professor of Theology at Yale Divinity, depicts the cross. He says it is *"the giving up of God's self in order not to give up on humanity...the arms of the crucified are open—a sign of space in God's self and an invitation for the enemy to come in."* The New Testament is clear: we considered God to be our enemy, but His arms were opened up to us.

My vision of God was pleasantly torn down and rebuilt, but this time on the foundation of the incarnate Son of God. The clarity of Christ shakes me with unmatched grace. Worship now transcends any previous height, as I taste His kindness. I no longer keep one eye open around Him to feel safe–His forgiveness eclipses any concern of harm.

This might challenge you. I imagine your passion for holiness might be reaching for the "but He..." aspects of your theology. Trust me, He isn't a careless Father. He invites us to attempt to exhaust His inexhaustible kindness, and it leads us to repentance. His trust in the transformational power of His grace shames our attempts to coerce holiness through punishment. He's not indifferent or irresponsible with sin–He's a Father who instead guides us with correction, and correction isn't punishment.

The mode of operation of Heaven is reconciliation, through the means of not counting our trespasses against us. This is how we feel the scandal of His grace. We can obsess over those who abuse grace, while God chooses instead to keep running out to meet them as they return home.

I don't claim to have it all worked out. I understand there's a mystery regarding certain passages of Scripture. I simply want to take seriously the authority Scripture gives to know God through Christ, and see to Him as the same yesterday, today, and forever.

Jesus overcame my deception in God's vengeful alter ego. I come to Him to be clothed and picked up, not embarrassed and punished. He dusts me off with a holy disregard for my mess, and He never threatens me. I expect His mercy every morning. My worst moments are opportunities to know His grace. I don't fear the retribution of a vengeful deity, because I wake up basking in His pleasure over me. His kindness has kept me from sin with far greater success than any threats of punishment ever did.

Question

In which areas of your life is Jesus inviting you to have a redeemed understanding of who He is?

Prayer

Jesus, I repent of seeing You wrongly, and I reconnect to seeing You rightly. Jesus, I lean into the truth of who You say You are, and who I know You to be. Your character is unending, and Your presence in my life is unmatched. I press past my insecurities and into Your promises. Jesus, You renew my mind daily—and You are constantly revealing more and more of Yourself to me. I am so thankful. I ask for You to pull down any flawed ways of seeing You. You're more kind than I know. Tear down any false images of You. You are the great redeemer. Amen.

Silence
2 minutes of sitting in silence being present to Jesus and yourself.

Presence

Holy Spirit lead me.
Holy Spirit sustain me.
Holy Spirit move through me.

Week Four
Day 25

Presence
Jesus, hold me. I desire to be comforted by Your Presence. When I am in Your arms, I know I am well. You satisfy me. You alone carry words of life. I cannot go on without You. My whole being thirsts to drink from Your living water. Jesus, Your embrace heals me. You're the Shepherd of my soul.

Silence
2 minutes of sitting in silence being present to Jesus and yourself.

Worship
Tell Jesus the place He has in your life and what He means to you.

Meditation

Isaiah 43: 1-2

Read it. Pray it. Ponder it.

I have called you by your name;

Psalm of the week 103

You are Mine. When you pass through the waters, I will be with you; And through the rivers, they shall not overflow you. When you walk through the fire, you shall not be burned, Nor shall the flame scorch you.

Scripture: Luke 24:13-35

¹³ Now that same day two of them were going to a village called Emmaus, about seven miles from Jerusalem. ¹⁴ They were talking with each other about everything that had happened. ¹⁵ As they talked and discussed these things with each other, Jesus himself came up and walked along with them; 16 but they were kept from recognizing him.

¹⁷ He asked them, "What are you discussing together as you walk along?"

They stood still, their faces downcast. ¹⁸ One of them, named Cleopas, asked him, "Are you the only one visiting Jerusalem who does not know the things that have happened there in these days?"

¹⁹ "What things?" he asked.

"About Jesus of Nazareth," they replied. "He was a prophet,powerful in word and deed before God and all the people. ²⁰ The chief priests and our rulers handed him over to be sentenced to death, and they crucified him; ²¹ but we had hoped that he was the one who was going to redeem Israel. And what is more, it is the third day since all this took place. ²² In addition, some of our women amazed us. They went to the tomb early this morning ²³ but didn't find his body. They came and told us that they had seen a vision of angels, who said he was alive. ²⁴ Then some of our companions went to the tomb and found it just as the women had said, but they did not see Jesus."

²⁵ He said to them, "How foolish you are, and how slow to believe all that the prophets have spoken! ²⁶ Did not the Messiah have to suffer these things and then enter his glory?" ²⁷ And beginning with Moses and all the Prophets,he explained to them what was said in all the Scriptures concerning himself.

²⁸ As they approached the village to which they were going, Jesus continued on as if he were going farther. ²⁹ But they urged him strongly, "Stay with us, for it is nearly evening; the day is almost over." So he went in to stay with them.

³⁰ When he was at the table with them, he took bread, gave thanks, broke it and began to give it to them. ³¹ Then their eyes were opened and they recognized him, and he disappeared from their sight. ³² They asked each other, "Were not our hearts burning within us while he talked with us on the road and opened the Scriptures to us?"

³³ They got up and returned at once to Jerusalem. There they found the Eleven and those with them, assembled together ³⁴ and saying, "It is true! The Lord has risen and has appeared to Simon." ³⁵ Then the two told what had happened on the way, and how Jesus was recognized by them when he broke the bread. (NIV)

Devotional: Illusion of A Distant God

I want to be close to God.

It's what I've wanted from the moment I experienced the

Holy Spirit. I was undone in all the right ways. God was present and I knew it. I wanted to maintain that same sense of closeness as much as possible. But in my passion, I unintentionally tried to earn God's closeness as a reward for my good living.

Distance with God started as it does for most.

I was having these intervals of experiencing God. One moment He was undeniably close, but then I would go a week or month without that sense of closeness again. The chasm between each experience of His closeness pushed me into believing God was far off until I had another one of these encounters again.

It was frustrating because I wanted to be near Him more than anything. I examined my life as a detective, searching for clues that would put me back on the trail to God. I would try to connect the dots to recreate the same results.

Here are the things I would ask myself if I felt God had become distant:

Did I fast?

Did I spend an hour in prayer?

Did I worship in the quiet with no one around?

Did I give something away?

Did I pray for someone?

Did someone pray for me?

I wanted to create a formula for being close to God. I fell into a trap. I defined God being close to me as a specific kind of experience–and if I wasn't having the same experience, I tried every trick I could to get it back. It started to feel exhausting.

One day I was reading the ending of the gospel of Luke. It's the passage where the disciples were walking with Jesus after He rose from the dead, but they didn't know it was Him. Jesus walked and talked with them, but they couldn't discern it was Him.

Have you ever thought about what that might mean?

I had preconceived ideas about what being close looked like. I assumed I would always be able to recognize when Jesus was with me. I assumed closeness to Jesus looked like being on my knees crying, or some other uncontrollable experience. After Jesus walks on the road with them, they invite Him in to share a meal–and Jesus breaks bread with them. It says, *"Their eyes were opened."* In one moment the disciples realized it was Jesus with them and they said, *"Did our hearts not burn within us?"*

These disciples were experiencing Jesus. Their hearts were burning within them, but their perceptions about God wouldn't allow them to fully experience Him. They could not yet recognize that it was Jesus in their midst–yet their hearts burned and had they listened, they would have known.

The distance was an illusion.

I read this scripture over and over again. I no longer wanted to earn God's nearness. I remembered His name is Emmanuel, "God with us". I knew that from then on, I had to be careful to not reverse in my mind what God had already revealed about Himself in Jesus.

God is with me.

He is with me. It's not because I am perfect, and it's not because I found the formula for drawing close to Him. It's because Jesus has torn down any wall of separation between us—and He gave us complete access to our Father. He has given us an irrevocable welcome into His presence.

Our Father is not far off. Jesus has brought us near to Him. The Cross is the declaration that God would rather die than be without us. Drawing close to our humanity does not violate His Godliness. Colossians says, *"It pleased the Father to dwell in bodily form."* We can think God is too holy to be close to us, and then we try to clean ourselves up for Him to be near. Well, Jesus debunks that. He is the friend of sinners. God didn't ask for the world to become whole before He decided to rescue us. God doesn't withhold His friendship until you become whole— His friendship is what makes you whole.

The New Testament gives us such great confidence that our Father is so close to us. He is not a distant God that is uninterested and reluctant. He is not unmoved by us. King David found he would become overwhelmed with God's loving thoughts about him as he worshipped, saying, *"Who is man that You are mindful of him?"*

Even when we're ignorant of His presence, He is with us. And even when we're not aware of Him, He continues to be mindful of us. God can't stop thinking about you.

Have you created or believed in any formula for earning God's that you need to repent from?

Prayer

Jesus, I'm in awe that You would choose to come close to me. Thank you for dismantling all my false perceptions of what it means to be in relationship with You–for you are the God that calls Himself Emmanuel. I pray that I would start to not only feel Your nearness in the "big" moments, but that my heart would burn within me as I recognize You walking with me in the "mundane" moments, too. Amen.

Silence

2 minutes of sitting in silence being present to Jesus and yourself.

Presence

Holy Spirit lead me.
Holy Spirit sustain me.
Holy Spirit move through me.

Week Four

Day 26

Presence

Jesus, hold me. I desire to be comforted by Your Presence. When I am in Your arms, I know I am well. You satisfy me. You alone carry words of life. I cannot go on without You. My whole being thirsts to drink from Your living water. Jesus, Your embrace heals me. You're the Shepherd of my soul.

Silence

2 minutes of sitting in silence being present to Jesus and yourself.

Worship

Tell Jesus the place He has in your life and what He means to you.

Isaiah 43: 1-2

Read it. Pray it. Ponder it.

I have called you by your name; You are Mine. When you pass through the waters, I will be with you; And through the rivers, they shall not overflow you. When you walk through the fire, you shall not be burned, Nor shall the flame scorch you.

Scripture: Romans 8:28

[28] And we know that God causes all things to work together for good to those who love God, to those who are called according to His purpose. (NASB)

Devotional: Blaming God

Christians have always wrestled with the problem of suffering in the world–and many have become professionals at blaming God for it. I was once counted among them. I was confused, and I lacked any other way of looking at suffering. The question suffering asks of the nature of God cannot be ignored–it's central to our understanding of God's nature.

These questions were deep, but my answers felt shallow.

I wondered: is the injustice of the world part of God's meticulous, sovereign plan?

Are we supposed to swallow our concerns, and chalk it all up to the unknowable mystery of God's will?

I think many people are confused about God's nature—and their conclusions make to the devil and God look similar.

Those initial questions lead us to even deeper concerns:

Why should we invest in making the world better if God is the one causing the suffering?

Why try to end poverty if it's part of His plan?

Why build hospitals, if sickness is God's divine will?

Have you ever wondered why nice Christian clichés like, "This is all part of God's plan," can feel empty and powerless in the midst of real suffering? They're actually doctrines in disguise, and they make it difficult to fall in love with God.

But if God is not the cause of our suffering, what's the other option?

The Bible is clear: we have a God who is all-powerful, and high above our circumstances. He's leading His creation toward His desired end. That—without a shadow of a doubt—is going to happen. Scripture is clear about it; His power isn't even in question. Scripture is clear about it; In the end, God wins.

So, why do bad things happen?

Evils like murder, torture, the victimization of children, or an unexpected sickness in the family make us doubt the sovereign goodness of God. It becomes tempting to assume God is somehow behind it all.

Logic leads us to only one conclusion: if God is all-powerful, then He is either causing these evils–or allowing them for some greater purpose. If God has a sovereign plan that He meticulously controls, there is no other explanation for why these sorts of injustices could contradict His love and goodness.

Eventually, we start to think God could allow something like cancer in a person's life–in order to teach the sick person noble qualities like humility, or endurance. Theology like this could lead us to believe God allowed an event like the September 11 attacks, in order for America to turn back to God and repent for their wrong ways. Tsunamis, earthquakes, and other natural disasters could be "acts of God" to serve as God's rebuke for our national and cultural sins. If God controls the world like this, then every evil must serve God's "higher way."

This worldview gives us security. If God is behind the wheel, then there are no bumps in the road, no wrong turns, and no detours that God didn't choose for us.

It feels logical to say, "God is in control". But I think it's more biblical to say that God is in charge.

If we believe "God is in control" like a watchmaker, it will keep us from who we are called to be in the world. I lived with this exact worldview–and I was afraid of God. I want to help you see another way–one that doesn't blame God for the suffering. You don't have to believe that He causes cancer, brings tsunamis, or makes you fail final exams to teach you a lesson.

But where do we begin?

First, let us address something we're quick to under-appreciate: our own free will.

I believe that God created us with free will–which means we can choose to do what is right or wrong. We're not just the product of our environment or circumstances. The Bible wouldn't hold us accountable for our decisions if we didn't have any real freedom. We're not marching robots.

Why do I believe we are truly free?

Love.

God wanted us to experience the reality of His nature. He wanted our world to know love–and in order to have genuine love, you need real freedom.

C.S. Lewis argues that in order for God to have a world of love, there must be an option to not choose Him. Love requires freedom or it wouldn't be love. The significance of this freedom cannot be overstated. This is the birthplace for the option of evil. Evil becomes possible when there's real freedom. Adam and Eve had the ability to choose to sin, or resist the devil. The option to make the wrong choice had to be present in order for there to be a real choice at all.

Well, doesn't that mean things might happen that God did not intend? Yes.

Does this feel risky? Yes.

The question isn't about whether this is too risky. It's about what kind of world is worth having. Does God want a world where love is possible? Yes. Therefore, He had to risk making a world where evil is possible. A world where people could choose the works of darkness over the works of light. Their potential for love was also their potential for evil.

In the garden, Adam and Eve were tempted by satan–and it's also where we see the first painful consequences of someone not making the right choice with their freedom.

This is where we see the beginnings of a cosmic war. Satan comes to persuade Adam and Eve into choosing evil over good. This changes things up for the human race, because they voluntarily gave up the pleasures of the garden and handed dominion for the earth over to the devil. Adam and Eve were told by God that if they ate of the forbidden fruit, they would surely die.

I don't know if you've noticed this, but they didn't die instantly. The death they welcomed into the world was the dominion of death over all Creation. This is the death that Christ comes to relinquish. The suffering introduced into the world was the consequence of misused freedom–it was not the arbitrary will of God.

Essentially, a world of harm had to be possible in order for a world of real love to exist. This story reveals that there's a devil who is against the will of God. This enemy is the provoker of perversion, and his influence betrays what is good and right about God's world. God never intended for Adam and Eve to fall, but He always knew it could happen.

"When God chose to make us truly free, He also chose not to be in control. He made the possibility of rejection real–and yet, He still created us anyway. The fall of Adam and Eve was not God's will or design. But it also wasn't something He was unprepared for! God's sovereignty means He will win over evil. But like a chess master, He has prepared many plans and contingencies. He will bring about His victory without overriding our freedom.

There is an enemy who is not an equal to God, but stands in opposition to Him. And this enemy continues to induce suffering upon our world by convincing humanity to use their authority and freedom in ways that violate God's good creation.

Now that we understand there is a war going on, let's look at the example of Jesus.

We must have a firm grip on Jesus as our perfect theology. Jesus is God. He is not one side of God–He is the definitive revelation of God. He is the cornerstone by which all thoughts about God are measured. If you've seen Jesus, then you've seen the Father. Any of our thoughts about God that are in conflict with what we see in the life of Jesus must be changed.

Therefore, we know what God thinks about human suffering by how Jesus responded to people.

Did He ascribe suffering to the meticulous, mysterious will of His Father?

Did He ever claim people died because they were being judged for their sin? Were the diseased experiencing God's divine purpose?

No.

Jesus heals the sick, casts out demons, and calms storms—and these miracles are described as Jesus *doing His Father's work.* His ministry reveals His Father, which means the sickness is not His Father's work. If it was, then healing the sick would mean He was in opposition to His Father. Acts 10:38 reveals that Jesus healed all who were oppressed of the devil—not by God, but by the devil.

The Apostle John tells us that Jesus came to destroy the works of the devil. The oppression, suffering, and evil in the world is exactly what Jesus came to destroy. Evil finds its origins in satan, not in God. The devil is the one stealing, killing, and destroying people, not God's mysterious will. The climax of Jesus destroying the works of the devil was the Cross. It disarmed the principalities, and defeated the devil. The church was always intended to manifest His victory when suffering occurs—not to call it God's work.

Paul teaches us that we're going to experience trials—things will happen that aren't according to God's will. This can only happen if God is in charge, but not in control. The confidence for the Christian comes as we understand Romans 8:28: God is still here in the world, working all things together for good.

This means some things we experience are not what He intends. But by being in charge, He works them out for us. There is no form of evil that cannot be conquered and transformed by God's sovereign will.

What the enemy intended for evil, God will turn for good.

Therefore, if something good comes out of something bad, it doesn't mean God first caused it. It reveals that God is so faithful and so good that He can transform our problems into blessings.

It's time to abandon the false comfort of thinking God is in control of everything.

When we recognize this, we no longer feel helpless and passive in the face of suffering. We confront it with Jesus's victory.

The bottom line is that we need to stop blaming God.

Question

What's your honest response to bad things happening?

_____

Prayer
Jesus, I repent for believing you have ever intended evil or pain to transpire in my life. I rest in the truth that you are a good and just friend who works out everything for my good. Jesus, I lean into you–even when it feels risky. My faith in you is what brings me closer to you–it does not lead me away. Jesus, I rest in your victorious nature. I ask for you to work all things together for my good. Amen.

Silence
2 minutes of sitting in silence being present to Jesus and yourself.

Presence
Holy Spirit lead me.
Holy Spirit sustain me.
Holy Spirit move through me.

Presence

Jesus, hold me. I desire to be comforted by Your Presence.
When I am in Your arms, I know I am well. You satisfy me.
You alone carry words of life. I cannot go on without You.
My whole being thirsts to drink from Your living water. Jesus,
Your embrace heals me. You're the Shepherd of my soul.

Silence

2 minutes of sitting in silence being present to Jesus and
yourself.

Worship

Tell Jesus the place He has in your life and what He means
to you.

Meditation

Isaiah 43: 1-2

Read it. Pray it. Ponder it.

**I have called you by your name;
You are Mine. When you pass
through the waters, I will be with
you; And through the rivers, they
shall not overflow you. When
you walk through the fire, you
shall not be burned, Nor shall
the flame scorch you.**

Scripture: Acts 10:38

[1] "Then Jesus was led by the Spirit into the wilderness to be
tempted by the devil." (NIV)

Devotional: A Pure Life

Jesus is a real human.

That's orthodoxy for you.

He wasn't "sort of" human. He was totally human, and totally God. We can't be scared of Jesus being fully man. The early Church was not afraid of this truth—and anyone who denied it was robustly challenged. The context of Christ's humanity helps us understand what the scripture means when it says Jesus *"learned obedience through the things He suffered."*

If we examine the life of Jesus, we quickly discover His relationship to the Holy Spirit. We discern His submission to this Spirit. Jesus lives a remarkable, pure life—and He does supernatural things. We witness a full and sustained measure of inner purity, and a masterful display of endless power, previously unknown to any human.

Jesus and other New Testament writers attribute this purity and power to the anointing of the Holy Spirit. The Gospels go out of their way to connect Jesus with the Spirit. They do this for many reasons. We know ancient Israel's growing hope, articulated by Isaiah, of a servant king who would have the Spirit of the Lord upon him to usher in the new creation. But there's another reason: it has to do with Jesus' role as the firstborn of new creation.

Jesus came to reveal what is possible for our human existence. He was the first of many. He wanted us to see God's dream for us. He came as the epitome of human life. He lived life with an openness to the Spirit, and by the empowerment by the Spirit. His purity set a new trajectory for human life. We're tempted think His example is beyond us. But as the firstborn of creation, He serves as our starting line.

Jesus prepares a way for us to live free from sin. A pure life is possible when a person is walking in the Spirit. One New Testament writer put it this way: if we walk in the Spirit we can deny the very lust that leads to sin. We witness Jesus, full of the Spirit, led into the wilderness to be tempted to sin. But He didn't fall to the temptation–and He left the wilderness in the power of the Spirit.

The Holy Spirit is an essential ingredient to our redeemed humanity. We become the humans God intends for us through a dependent relationship upon the Spirit. We cannot have the fruit of the Spirit without a conscious openness to the Spirit.

I say "conscious openness" because this kind of life involves a choice to maintain an ongoing awareness of the Spirit. We have to begin organizing our life around this reality, surrendering whatever would put us at odds with Him. We begin laying down control of our life, and we lay down our false strategies for finding life. This means we begin to consult the wisdom of the Spirit over our best attempts to find hope, love, joy, and peace. We begin to consider Him in our choices, recognizing He will constantly affirm the identity given to us by the Father. The Spirit solidifies our true self–and as a new creation modelled after Jesus, we have no need for sin.

It's fascinating how quickly we can ignore the Spirit. I don't think I can find a person who would look at pornogrpahy with their mom or dad next to them. The conscious awareness of a good parent adjusts our behavior for the better. If we could remember to live conscious of the Holy Spirit's presence in our lives, we would adjust our behavior away from destructive tendencies. We would begin living out of the purity given to us by Jesus. We only sin intentionally when we ignore the very present help of the Spirit.

The Holy Spirit was essential for Jesus to live a pure life. He was tempted in all ways, but without sin—and we can follow His example. We can live a pure life by the empowering presence of the Holy Spirit. Jesus said the Spirit will take what is His and make it known to us. The Holy Spirit is actively looking to make real in our lives what was real in Jesus' life. This means sharing in the miraculous power and sustained purity of Jesus.

Question

How does the ever-present reality of the Holy Spirit cause you to change the way you live today?

Prayer

Jesus, I am alive to Your Spirit. It is essential to my relationship with You. I intentionally welcome Your purity and I welcome Your Spirit to make this possible in my life. I turn my back on destructive tendencies, and I focus on the path of Your righteousness. Holy Spirit, lead me past temptation and into the Kingdom of God. I ask You to uproot any resistance I might have to the Spirit. Jesus, teach me to live open and led by the Spirit. Amen.

Silence

2 minutes of sitting in silence being present to Jesus and yourself.

Presence

Holy Spirit lead me.
Holy Spirit sustain me.
Holy Spirit move through me.

Presence

Jesus, hold me. I desire to be comforted by Your Presence. When I am in Your arms, I know I am well. You satisfy me. You alone carry words of life. I cannot go on without You. My whole being thirsts to drink from Your living water. Jesus, Your embrace heals me. You're the Shepherd of my soul.

Silence

2 minutes of sitting in silence being present to Jesus and yourself.

Worship

Tell Jesus the place He has in your life and what He means to you.

Meditation

Isaiah 43: 1-2

Read it. Pray it. Ponder it.

I have called you by your name; You are Mine. When you pass through the waters, I will be with you; And through the rivers, they shall not overflow you. When you walk through the fire, you shall not be burned, Nor shall the flame scorch you.

Scripture: Genesis 22:1-13

[1] After these things God tested Abraham and said to him, "Abraham!" And he said, "Here I am." [2] He said, "Take your son, your only son Isaac, whom you love, and go to the land of Moriah, and offer him there as a burnt offering on one of

169

the mountains of which I shall tell you." ³ So Abraham rose early in the morning, saddled his donkey, and took two of his young men with him, and his son Isaac. And he cut the wood for the burnt offering and arose and went to the place of which God had told him. ⁴ On the third day Abraham lifted up his eyes and saw the place from afar. ⁵ Then Abraham said to his young men, "Stay here with the donkey; I and the boy will go over there and worship and come again to you." ⁶ And Abraham took the wood of the burnt offering and laid it on Isaac his son. And he took in his hand the fire and the knife. So they went both of them together. ⁷ And Isaac said to his father Abraham, "My father!" And he said, "Here I am, my son." He said, "Behold, the fire and the wood, but where is the lamb for a burnt offering?" ⁸ Abraham said, "God will provide for himself the lamb for a burnt offering, my son." So they went both of them together.

⁹ When they came to the place of which God had told him, Abraham built an altar there and laid the wood in order and bound Isaac his son and laid him on the altar, on top of the wood. ¹⁰ Then Abraham reached out his hand and took the knife to slaughter his son. ¹¹ But the angel of the Lord called to him from heaven and said, "Abraham, Abraham!" And he said, "Here I am." ¹² He said, "Do not lay your hand on the boy or do anything to him, for now I know that you fear God, seeing you have not withheld your son, your only son, from me." ¹³ And Abraham lifted up his eyes and looked, and behold, behind him was a ram, caught in a thicket by his horns. And Abraham went and took the ram and offered it up as a burnt offering instead of his son.

Devotional: Uncontested in Our Heart

Have you ever really thought about the story of Abraham

and Isaac?

It's a story about a man going up a mountain to make a required sacrifice before God. Isaac was the promised child, embodying all that God promised Abraham. Abraham didn't take Ishmael up the mountain–this was the "chosen" son. Isaac was the result of Abraham following the promise God's way. Abraham wasn't being punished for some dis-obedience–yet God asked Abraham to sacrifice Isaac. The promise had to be put on the altar.

We need to remember that God wanted Isaac to be born. It was part of His whole plan. God would use Abraham as a father to the nations. Abraham had not handled his calling perfectly–nobody does. But this moment on the mountain was a reflection of Abraham's faithfulness, not a course-cor-rection. Abraham's unfolding promise needed one final piece.

There's a feeling of stability that comes when you know you are stewarding all God has given to you. You're overcom-ing the routine challenges against your call to faithfulness. There are still mistakes, restarts, and pride you must submit along the way–but you start to anticipate your dream right around the corner. You see the top of the mountain you've been climbing, and it looks good.

It's in this moment God teaches you a lesson to save you from destruction.

He's not asking for a sacrifice because you've done it wrong. On the contrary–it is because you've done it right. God, in His mercy, is making sure that you're not consumed with your promise, but with Him.

If we're going to fear anything, He wants us to fear losing our relationship with Him more than fearing the loss of our promises.

God is telling you that your gift or promise is not the most important thing about you. The most important thing about you is that you're given to Him. God wants to solidify His place in the center of your life.

He doesn't want to compete with the promises. He knows if our gifts, talents, and promises take His seat, they will destroy us. If they become the most important thing about us, then we've gained the world–but lost our souls.

God wants to dwell in our hearts uncontested. He wants us to pursue Him with everything before we pursue anything else. Our identity isn't in our talents or promises. We're nothing before we are His. We are first known by our love for Him. We meet the world not as people with great skills, achievements, and dreams–but first as people who are given to God.

God can speak to us as we carry our Isaac up the mountain to be sacrificed. We will hear God speak when we anchor ourselves to Him, and are willing to lay our gifts and promises down. However, if we use our sacrifice as another way to feel important, we will actually end up killing our Isaac instead of simply being willing to do it.

Our promises are kept alive when we give ourselves to God first. The story doesn't end with Abraham killing his son, Isaac. God provides the sacrifice, and Abraham receives Isaac back as though he were resurrected from the dead. Abraham isn't clenching his hands proclaiming, "God gave him to me! I don't need to sacrifice him." Our promises find their origin in God. They become blessings, not curses, when we surrender them to Him. We won't be required to kill them if we're willing to sacrifice them at any time. They can never be the first thing our heart is given to.

Our dreams are only as safe as they are submitted to intimacy with God.

We are first given to God.

Question

How do you make sure your heart is given to God first?

_____

Prayer

Jesus, Here I am; my life is yours. I surrender my dreams, ambitions, and pursuits to be one with you. Jesus, You are the one I love. My greatest desire is to be one with You. Jesus, I long to be in Your presence, and it is in Your presence that I am made whole. I am devoted to seeing Your kingdom come, and I am regularly encountering You daily. I am living a life laid down so that You may be glorified over and over. It is in your name I pray. Amen.

Silence

2 minutes of sitting in silence being present to Jesus and yourself.

Presence

Holy Spirit lead me.
Holy Spirit sustain me.
Holy Spirit move through me.

Notes

Chapter Two: Life As A Disciple
Matthew 10:25 (ESV)
For further study on discipleship read:
All of Dallas Willard's books, The Complete Book of Discipleship:
On Being and Making Followers of Christ by Bill Hull (NavPress;
Annotated edition edition (November 6, 2006),

Chapter Three: The Practice
A. W. Tozer, The Pursuit of God: Moody Publishers; Reissue edition
(April 1, 2015)

Bill Johnson, Hosting His Presence: Unveiling Heaven's Agenda:
Destiny Image; 38030th edition (May 15, 2012)

1 Timothy 4:8 (ESV)
1 Corinthians 9:25-27 (NLT)
Phillipians 4:9 (NIV)
Matthew 7:4 (ESV)

Dallas Willard, Renovation of the Heart: Putting On the Character
of Christ: NavPress; Anniversary edition (June 28, 2012)

Chapter Four: Posture of Heart
Richard Foster, Celebration of Discipline: The Path to Spiritual
Growth: HarperOne; Anniversary, Special edition (February 13,
2018)

Jean Guyon, Experiencing The Depths of Jesus Christ: Christian
Books Pub House; 3rd edition (June 1, 1981)

Dallas Willard, The Divine Conspiracy: Rediscovering Our Hidden
Life In God: HarperOne (February 6, 2009)

Day 01: Silence and Solitude
Ruth Hayley Barton, The Invitation to Silence and Solitude, IVP Books;
Expanded edition (October 1, 2010)

Day 02: Simplicity
Richard Foster, Celebration of Discipline, HarperOne; Anniversary, Special
edition (February 13, 2018)

Day 03: The Three Temptations
Hebrews 4:15 (NIV)
Mark 1:11 (NKJV)
John 14:30 (ESV)

Day 04: Rest for the Soul
Kallistos Ware, The Orthodox Way, St Vladimir's Seminary Press (July 1,
2012)

Day 10: Waiting for the Spirit
John G. Lake, The Flow of the Spirit, Whitaker House; Reissue, Repackage
of Living in God's Power edition (July 10, 2018)

Day 12: Death to Self
Dietrich Bonhoeffer, Costly Grace, IVP Connect; 6th Studies for Individuals
or Groups ed. edition (June 1, 2002)

Dallas Willard, Life without Lack: Living in the Fullness of Psalm 23: Thomas
Nelson (February 26, 2019)

Day 13: Thirsting After God
A.W Tozer, Mornings with Tozer: Daily Devotional Readings, Moody Publishers; Revised edition (May 1, 2015)

Day 14: Well-Kept Heart
Dallas Willard, The Renovation of the Heart: Putting on the Character of
Christ, NavPress; Anniversary edition (June 28, 2012)

Day 19: Living in a Bubble
Bubble Boy. Directed by Blair Hayes. Performances by Jake Gyllenhall.
Touchstone Pictures, Buena Vista Pictures. August 24, 2001.(Bubble Boy)

Day 20: Part of the Solution
Bill Johnson, When Heaven Invades Earth, Destiny Image Publishers (Jan-
uary 1, 2005)

Day 21: Love One Another
Thomas Merton, No Man Is an Island, Mariner Books; First edition (Octo-

ber 28, 2002)

Day 22: Destroying the Works of the Devil
Jon Tyson, "Life of a Disciple" Sermon Bethel Church Redding, California 2019

Day 24: The Revelation of God in Christ
A. W. Tozer, The Knowledge of the Holy: HarperCollins / 1992 / Hardcover

Miroslav Volf, Exclusion & Embrace: A Theological Exploration of Identity, Otherness, and Reconciliation: Abingdon Press; 1st edition (December 1, 1996)

Day 26: Blaming God
C.S. Lewis, Mere Christianity: HarperOne; Revised & Enlarged edition (April 21, 2015)

Thanks

My wife, Lana, for you constant belief in me. Your enduring sacrifice to go on this spiritual journey with me. You're my dream come true. I love you.

Solomon and Pearl, for giving me the gift of being your Dad. I wrote this for you. I love you.

Mom and Dad, for making a way for me to dream since I was a little boy.

Joelle Ballweg, Irvin Hamilton, and Claire Christensen, for you helping turning this idea into a reality.

Connor Shram, for being a great friend and making this book better with your editing genius.

Tribe Young Adults, for going on this wild ride of building a community that encounters God and becomes like Jesus.

Bethel Church and BSSM, for giving me a chance, teaching me what it means to be a spiritual son, and inspiring me to always be hungry for the presence of God.

About the Author

Chris Cruz serves on the Church Leadership Team at Bethel Church in Redding, CA as the Young Adults Pastor. Originally from New Jersey, Chris moved to Redding to attend Bethel School of Supernatural Ministry (BSSM) in 2007. After graduating he worked as a Revival Group Pastor at BSSM for 7 years. After BSSM, Chris helped start Tribe Young Adults. They exist to call young adults to encounter God so that, together, we can see heaven and earth unite.

Chris is passionate about knowing the Holy Spirit and Spiritual Formation. He is devoted to seeing heaven and earth become one. He teaches leaders and churches about the ways of the Kingdom and the priority of experiencing God's Presence. Chris and his wife Lana live in Redding, CA with their son Solomon and daughter Pearl.

Follow Chris on Instagram: @chriscruz

Printed in Great Britain
by Amazon

37392789R00102